Supersized Cookies for Over-th

BIG
YUM

Chloe Joy Sexton, Creator of BluffCakes Confections

PAGE STREET
PUBLISHING CO.

PAGE STREET
PUBLISHING CO.

First published in 2023 by
Page Street Publishing Co.
27 Congress Street, Suite 1511
Salem, MA 01970
www.pagestreetpublishing.com

Distributed by Macmillan, sales in Canada by The Canadian Manda Group.

27   26   25   24   23   1   2   3   4   5

ISBN-13: 978-1-64567-967-7
ISBN-10: 1-64567-967-5

Library of Congress Control Number: 2022949669

Cover and book design by Emma Hardy for Page Street Publishing Co.
Photography by Alison Stukenborg

Printed and bound in the United States

For Her,
Jenny Wren, my silly bird,
my mother and the one who gave me this voice.
I did it.

TABLE OF

CONTENTS

INTRODUCTION

When I first embarked on my giant cookie journey, I'd spent my entire professional life focusing on my career and treating my passion for baking as a "silly little hobby" on the sidelines of my "real path." Little did I know . . .

Some of my earliest memories of baking are with my mother and Martha Stewart. My mother, Jenny Wren, and I would watch hours of Martha stacking cakes, making ganache or arranging flowers from her garden. To me, she embodied everything I learned to love about baking. Baking is an art made to be shared and a creative outlet that began when I was 12 years old and has lasted my entire life. My mother was always an artist in many forms, but I never had an artistic bone in my body. I could watch her design jewelry, paint or sculpt all in one day, and I simply never inherited her skills. The day I took up baking, I knew I had found my medium. After my having been a very high-strung, competitive child obsessed with winning awards and high test scores, baking became my escape from my own perfectionism. Was it pretty? No? Who cares, if it tastes amazing?

At 21 years old, I was a news producer in Memphis, Tennessee. I worked from midnight to early morning and hardly existed during daylight hours. What little time I spent awake when the sun was still up, I spent baking. Every time I baked, I would bring the results to my news station team. News people aren't like regular people. If something I made was a baking flop, they were going to tell me to my face. Every day I spent working in news, I dreamed of trying the next recipe. I jotted down ideas for recipes with new flavor combinations during the commercial breaks of my newscasts. I began to realize that maybe my dream wasn't this job, but instead this "little hobby" that brought me more joy than anything. I still wasn't ready to walk away from the career I had worked so hard for, but I let myself dream.

I began sharing my baking on Instagram and eventually on TikTok and Facebook. My work began gaining me DMs of potential customers asking whether they could purchase what I was sharing. I hadn't really considered that social media alone could take my baking from hobby to side business, but I started taking so many custom orders that almost every spare moment outside work, I found myself baking and delivering. I decided to leave the newsy nightcrawler life.

It was my husband, Tyler, who pushed me to the next step. Days before we flew to Jamaica to get married, he sat me down to give me my wedding present: BluffCakes. He had spent weeks finding a graphic designer to make me a logo, building a website to share my recipes and accept custom orders and even making me my very first business cards that read "Chloe Sexton, Baker and Owner of BluffCakes." I cried. Obviously, I cried. From the very beginning, he saw what this meant to me, what baking did for me and the joy it brought me, and here he was saying, "Do this! I believe in you. You're better than you even know. You can do this."

Little did I know that the universe would push me into that leap I was too scared to take.

In a midpandemic turn of fate, I found myself unexpectedly jobless while pregnant, during the holidays and having just bought a house. To add more to how horrible this timing was, my mother was fighting brain cancer for a third time, and I was her sole caregiver. I was the most scared I've ever been in my life. After screaming and crying and staring at the walls for a few hours, I knew what I had to do. I began baking. I started with my faithful local customers, but I knew the holidays would pass and demand would die down. I began experimenting with an idea I'd played with before: giant cookies.

All along, I was sharing my life and baking with my growing social following. I knew that if I could just create something shelf-stable, delicious and shippable, then I could reach them, too.

And so the giant cookie journey began. I didn't just want to make any cookies, I wanted them to have wild, indulgent and exciting flavors. I wanted to watch people's eyes widen when I said words like "a giant chocolate chip cookie with pecans and then stuffed with maple bourbon pecans and iodized salted caramels."

I shared that silly little journey with my small social media following until it grew and grew and I found myself feeding an army of "Cookie Monsters" rooting me on through all my trials, tribulations and successes. From my kitchen to rented commercial kitchens to opening my family's bakery—I wasn't just sharing a hobby anymore, I was leaning into what I knew was my dream all along but I'd never had the confidence to chase.

I created these cookies while pregnant, through a pandemic and while eventually losing my mother to her 11-year battle with brain cancer. BluffCakes Confections became my husband's full-time job and my family's greatest adventure. Sacrifices, struggle and success are all deeply rooted in the story of my baking, and learning to take risks is exemplified in each giant cookie recipe.

My bakery is proof that people all over the world are ready to try crazy, indulgent flavors packed into giant cookies. In this book, you'll find cookies that range from family favorite flavors to giant, brightly colored treats packed with colorful cereal and stuffed with marshmallows, or a cowboy cookie packed with pecans, chocolate chips and an entire brownie stuffed in the middle. These cookies are adventurous, indulgent and guaranteed to pleasantly shock anyone you choose to share them with—if you share them at all.

This book is for all the Cookie Monsters who watched my wild, scary, delicious adventure and cheered me on. Bake these cookies and bring them along for all of your own delicious adventures.

CHAPTER 1:
CHOCOLATE & CHUNKY

Chocolate will always have my heart. It's the only flavor of cake I want on every birthday and the first thing I reached for when I was pregnant with Theodore and the cravings hit. I truly believe that almost every dessert can be made even better with just a little chocolate. In this chapter, you'll find some of my favorite combinations of savory, sweet, minty, thick and stuffed chocolate cookies.

Chocolate was the first kind of cookie I ever experimented with stuffing and baking BIG and the debut flavor of BluffCakes Bakery. The initial concept was taking my favorite candy, a Reese's peanut butter cup, and turning it into a cookie. I took my favorite chocolate cookie dough, stuffed it with peanut butter and sprinkled it with a pinch of flaky iodized salt for that salty-sweet finish. The result was divine. It has since stayed a staple on our menu.

MEXICAN CHOCOLATE COOKIES

Yields 8 giant cookies

This giant chocolate cookie comes with a kick—thick, fluffy Mexican chocolate flavor with just a little spice. I'd be lying if I said that my first attempt at nailing this cookie was a success. Thankfully, my bakery right hand, Jasmine, was there to be blatantly honest. "More cinnamon . . . more . . . *more*. Now, some chili powder." With each addition, I got nervous, but the result was, in my husband's words, "The best chocolate cookie I've ever had." Clearly, I won't doubt Jasmine again.

¾ cup (150 g) granulated sugar

¾ cup (169 g) light brown sugar

¾ cup (1½ sticks [170 g]) noniodized salted butter, at room temperature

2 large eggs

2 large egg yolks

3½ cups (438 g) all-purpose flour

½ cup (55 g) unsweetened cocoa powder

2 tsp (12 g) iodized salt

1 tsp baking powder

1 tsp baking soda

2 tsp (5 g) ground cinnamon

1 tsp Mexican chili powder

1¼ cups (219 g) chocolate chips

In a stand mixer fitted with the paddle attachment, or a large bowl using a handheld mixer, combine the granulated sugar, brown sugar and butter. Mix at medium speed until creamed, about 2 minutes. Scrape the mixture from the sides and paddle/beaters with a rubber spatula, then mix again until fully incorporated. This is complete when your mixture is light, fluffy and off-white.

Add the eggs and egg yolks, then mix until just combined.

Into a separate bowl, sift together your flour, cocoa powder, salt, baking powder, baking soda, cinnamon and Mexican chili powder. Then add the flour mixture to your wet mixture in three parts, making sure to scrape the bowl before each dry addition, to clear the butter from the sides of the bowl.

Turn your mixer setting to "Stir" and slowly add the chocolate chips, or turn it off and, using a rubber spatula, fold them in.

Cover your bowl with plastic wrap and chill in the refrigerator for 20 to 30 minutes, or until the dough is cold but still shapeable. While the dough is chilling, preheat the oven to 375°F (190°C). Line two baking sheets with parchment paper.

You can separate the chilled dough into eight equal-sized balls or use a kitchen scale and weigh them all to about 6 ounces (170 g) each. Place 3 inches (8 cm) apart on your prepared pans.

Bake for 10 to 12 minutes, or until they reach your ideal firmness. Remove from the oven. Let them rest on the pans for about 10 minutes before serving.

THE THICC MINT

This cookie is a childhood favorite reimagined. As a former Girl Scout myself, I hold some of the happiest memories of hoarding freezerfuls of this classic flavor well past cookie-selling season. My mother was my Girl Scout leader, and my grandmother was hers as a child. You could say selling cookies runs in my blood. I spent many a sunny Florida day as a kid with a gaggle of other green- and brown-clad little girls at a pop-up table outside grocery stores, pushing Tagalongs® and Samoas®.

This cookie is thicker and mintier than ever before with a delicious chocolate dough you'll want to eat right out of the bowl . . . but you didn't hear that from me.

¾ cup (150 g) granulated sugar

¾ cup (169 g) light brown sugar

¾ cup (1½ sticks [170 g]) unsalted butter, at room temperature

2 large eggs

2 large egg yolks

2 tsp (10 ml) peppermint extract

3½ cups (438 g) all-purpose flour

½ cup (55 g) unsweetened cocoa powder

1 tsp iodized salt

1 tsp baking powder

1 tsp baking soda

1 cup (170 g) mint chocolate candy chunks

½ cup (88 g) chocolate chips

In a stand mixer fitted with the paddle attachment, or a large bowl using a handheld mixer, combine the granulated sugar, brown sugar and butter. Mix at medium speed until creamed, about 2 minutes. Scrape the mixture from the sides and paddle/beaters with a rubber spatula, then mix again until fully incorporated. This is complete when your mixture is light, fluffy and off-white.

Add the eggs and egg yolks, then mix until just combined. Once you've scraped the sides of your bowl, add your peppermint extract and stir just a few times.

Into a separate bowl, sift together your flour, cocoa powder, salt, baking powder and baking soda, and then add the flour mixture to your wet mixture in three parts, making sure to scrape the bowl before each dry addition, to clear the butter from the sides of the bowl.

Turn your mixer setting to "Stir" and slowly add the mint chocolate chunks and chocolate chips, or turn it off and, using a rubber spatula, fold them in.

Cover your bowl with plastic wrap and chill in the refrigerator for 20 to 30 minutes, or until the dough is cold but still shapeable. While the dough is chilling, preheat the oven to 375°F (190°C). Line two baking sheets with parchment paper.

You can separate the chilled dough into eight equal-sized balls or use a kitchen scale and weigh them all to about 6 ounces (170 g) each. Place 3 inches (8 cm) apart on your prepared pans. Bake for 10 to 12 minutes, or until they reach your ideal firmness. Remove from the oven. Let them rest on the pans for about 10 minutes before digging in.

DEATH BY PIECES

Yields 7 to 8 giant cookies

My first true love: peanut butter. Then came my husband and he's great and all, but have you ever had chocolate and peanut better *together*?! This cookie is all of that and more—fudgy chocolate cookie dough packed with chocolate chips and Reese's Pieces™. The perfect amount of peanut butter and chocolate have a touch of iodized salt to bring your sweet and savory dreams to life in one giant cookie. A very pregnant Chloe made this recipe at the height of my cravings, and it quickly became a friends—and family—shared craving.

¾ cup (150 g) granulated sugar

¾ cup (169 g) light brown sugar

½ cup (1 stick [114 g]) unsalted butter

2 large eggs

1 large egg yolk

3½ cups (438 g) all-purpose flour

½ cup (55 g) unsweetened cocoa powder

2 tsp (12 g) iodized salt

1 tbsp (14 g) baking powder

1 tsp baking soda

1¼ cups (219 g) semisweet chocolate chips

½ cup (100 g) Reese's Pieces or similar candies

In a stand mixer fitted with the paddle attachment, or a large bowl using a handheld mixer, combine the granulated sugar, brown sugar and butter. Mix at medium-high speed until creamed, about 2 minutes. Scrape the mixture from the sides and paddle/beaters with a rubber spatula, then mix again until fully incorporated. This is complete when your mixture is light, fluffy and off-white.

Add the eggs and egg yolk, then mix until just combined.

Into a separate bowl, sift together your flour, cocoa powder, salt, baking powder and baking soda, then add the flour mixture to your wet mixture in three parts, making sure to scrape the bowl before each dry addition, to clear the butter from the sides of the bowl.

Turn off your mixer and, using a rubber spatula, fold your chocolate chips and Reese's Pieces into the dough.

Cover your bowl with plastic wrap and chill in the refrigerator for 30 minutes, or until the dough is cold but still shapeable. While the dough is chilling, preheat the oven to 375°F (190°C). Line two baking sheets with parchment paper.

Using your kitchen scale, form the chilled dough into balls anywhere from 6.5 to 6.8 ounces (184 to 193 g), or divide it into eight equal-sized balls. Place 3 inches (8 cm) apart on your prepared pans. Bake for 12 to 14 minutes, or until they reach your ideal firmness. Remove from the oven. Let your cookies rest on the pans for 5 to 10 minutes before serving.

CHOCOLATE BOURBON PECAN

If you walked into our home and glanced into the dining room, you'd see a large hutch displaying dozens of rare bourbons. No, they're not mine; they're my husband's, and I'm not even allowed to touch them. The flavors I'm rarely permitted to touch are the inspiration behind this cookie. Paired with rich cocoa flavor and iodized salty pecans, this is the perfect cookie to snack on beside a glass of your husband's treasured small batch.

¾ cup (150 g) granulated sugar

¾ cup (169 g) light brown sugar

¾ cup (1½ sticks [170 g]) unsalted butter, at room temperature

2 large eggs

2 large egg yolks

2 tsp (10 ml) bourbon emulsion (available from bakery supply shops or online)

3½ cups (438 g) all-purpose flour

½ cup (55 g) unsweetened cocoa powder

1 tsp iodized salt

1 tbsp (14 g) baking powder

1 tsp baking soda

½ cup (88 g) chocolate chips

½ cup (55 g) roughly chopped roasted and iodized salted pecans

In a stand mixer fitted with the paddle attachment, or a large bowl using a handheld mixer, combine the granulated sugar, brown sugar and butter. Mix at medium-high speed until creamed, about 2 minutes. Scrape the mixture from the sides and paddle/beaters with a rubber spatula, then mix again until fully incorporated. This is complete when your mixture is light, fluffy and off-white.

Add the eggs, egg yolks and bourbon emulsion, then mix until just combined.

Into a separate bowl, sift together your flour, cocoa powder, salt, baking powder and baking soda, then add the flour mixture to your wet mixture in three parts, making sure to scrape the bowl before each dry addition, to clear the butter from the sides of the bowl.

Turn off your mixer and, using a rubber spatula, fold in your chocolate chips and pecans. Cover your bowl with plastic wrap and chill in the refrigerator for 30 minutes, or until the dough is cold but still shapeable. While the dough is chilling, preheat the oven to 375°F (190°C). Line two baking sheets with parchment paper.

You can separate the chilled dough into eight equal-sized balls or use a kitchen scale and weigh them all to about 6 ounces (170 g) each. Place 3 inches (8 cm) apart on your prepared pans. Bake for 12 to 14 minutes, or until they reach your ideal firmness. Remove from the oven. Let your cookies rest on the pans for 5 to 10 minutes, then serve.

PISTACHIO DARK CHOCOLATE

Yields 6 to 8 giant cookies

Salty. Sweet. Nutty. Are we describing me or a delicious chocolate cookie? Pistachio pudding, pistachio chocolate tarts, roasted and iodized salted pecans, pistachio gelato—I could eat any of these in copious amounts. The secret to giving this cookie its extra *oomph* is the pistachio extract— you simply can't go without it.

½ cup (100 g) granulated sugar

¾ cup (169 g) light brown sugar

¾ cup (1½ sticks [170 g]) unsalted butter, at room temperature

2 large eggs

1 large egg yolk

1 tsp pistachio extract

3½ cups (438 g) all-purpose flour

¼ cup (32 g) cornstarch

1 tsp iodized salt

1 tbsp (14 g) baking powder

1 tsp baking soda

1 cup (175 g) roughly chopped dark chocolate

½ cup (62 g) roughly chopped, iodized salted pistachios

In a stand mixer fitted with the paddle attachment, or a large bowl using a handheld mixer, combine the granulated sugar, brown sugar and butter. Mix at high speed until creamed, about 2 minutes. Scrape the mixture from the sides and paddle/beaters with a rubber spatula, then mix again until fully incorporated. This is complete when your mixture is light, fluffy and off-white.

Add the eggs, egg yolk and pistachio extract, then mix until just combined.

Into a separate bowl, sift together your flour, cornstarch, salt, baking powder and baking soda, then add the flour mixture to your wet mixture in three parts, making sure to scrape the bowl before each dry addition, to clear the butter from the sides of the bowl.

Turn your mixer setting to "Stir" and slowly add the dark chocolate and pistachios, or turn it off and, using rubber spatula, fold them in.

Cover your bowl with plastic wrap and chill in the refrigerator for 20 to 30 minutes, or until the dough is cold but still shapeable. While the dough is chilling, preheat the oven to 375°F (190°C). Line two baking sheets with parchment paper.

You can separate the chilled dough into eight equal-sized balls or use a kitchen scale and weigh them all to about 6 ounces (170 g) each. Place 3 inches (8 cm) apart on your prepared pans. Bake for 10 to 12 minutes, or until they reach your ideal firmness. Remove from the oven. Let them rest on the pans for about 10 minutes before digging in.

STUFFED S'MORES COOKIES

Yields 7 to 8 giant cookies

As a child growing up in the sweltering Florida heat, I had never experienced a s'more. When my mother and I packed up and moved to the Deep South, I can distinctly remember the first fall camping trip with friends where I learned how to perfectly char a marshmallow so it would melt your chocolate and squeeze between the graham cracker walls perfectly. Minus the bonfire, this cookie packs all the same flavor and nostalgia with a sneaky marshmallow center.

¾ cup (150 g) granulated sugar

¾ cup (169 g) light brown sugar

¾ cup (1½ sticks [170 g]) unsalted butter, at room temperature

2 large eggs

2 large egg yolks

3½ cups (438 g) all-purpose flour

½ cup (55 g) unsweetened cocoa powder

1 tsp iodized salt

1 tbsp (14 g) baking powder

1 tsp baking soda

1 cup (175 g) semisweet chocolate chips

1 cup (45 g) lightly crushed graham crackers

8 Jet-Puffed Marshmallow Bites S'mores Flavored Coated Marshmallows™

In a stand mixer fitted with the paddle attachment, or a large bowl using a handheld mixer, combine the granulated sugar, brown sugar and butter. Mix at medium-high speed until creamed, about 2 minutes. Scrape the mixture from the sides and paddle/beaters with a rubber spatula, then mix again until fully incorporated.

Add the eggs and egg yolks, then mix until just combined.

Into a separate bowl, sift together your flour, cocoa powder, salt, baking powder and baking soda, then add the flour mixture to your wet mixture in three parts, making sure to scrape the bowl before each dry addition, to clear the butter from the sides of the bowl.

Turn off your mixer and, with a rubber spatula, fold in the chocolate chips and crushed graham crackers.

Cover your bowl with plastic wrap and chill in the refrigerator for 30 minutes, or until the dough is cold but still shapeable. While the dough is chilling, preheat the oven to 375°F (190°C). Line two baking sheets with parchment paper.

After the dough has chilled, divide it into eight balls or weigh to roughly 6 ounces (170 g) each. Using a large spoon or your fingers, press into the middle of a cookie dough ball to create a small space into which to place one marshmallow. Then, fold the surrounding cookie dough around the marshmallow and roll back into a ball. Repeat to fill the other dough balls.

Place four or five filled balls 3 inches (8 cm) apart on the prepared baking pans and lightly press on the top of each dough ball. Bake your cookies for 12 to 14 minutes, or until firm with slightly golden edges. Let them rest on the pans before serving.

CHAPTER 2:
PIECE OF CAKE

"If you make giant cookies . . . Why is your bakery called Bluff*cakes*?" Because cake was the beginning of everything. After years of baking at home, sharing only with family and friends, I finally created an Instagram just for my recent cake- and cupcake-decorating endeavors. We put down roots in Memphis, Tennessee (the *bluff* city), and I wanted my account to express my love for both my city and my baking.

Within a year, my evenings after work were full of custom cake, cupcake and especially cookie orders. My love for cake launched my desire to make big, fluffy, cakey cookies you couldn't find anywhere else. I took it a step further and started stuffing wildly indulgent flavors inside those cookies. These recipes bring some of my favorite cakes to life in giant cookie form.

RED VELVET CHOCOLATE HAZELNUT STUFFED COOKIES

Yields 8 giant cookies

This is one of the most satisfying stuffed cookies to crack open. When I first began experimenting with giant cookies and all the possibilities of what could be stuffed inside of them, I dreamed of making a big, cakey cookie that could be cracked open to reveal a melty chocolate surprise. This cookie made that dream come true! This is a thick, indulgent red velvet cookie packed with white chocolate chips with a sweet surprise—a gooey, melted, chocolaty, hazelnutty center. You're going to want a glass of milk with this one.

Center

1 (7.7 oz [220-g]) jar chocolate hazelnut spread (I use Nutella®)

Cookie Dough

¾ cup (150 g) granulated sugar

¾ cup (169 g) light brown sugar

¾ cup (1½ sticks [170 g]) unsalted butter, at room temperature

2 large eggs

2 large egg yolks

1 tbsp (15 ml) red velvet emulsion (available from bakery supply shops or online)

3 to 4 drops red food coloring, or as desired

3½ cups (438 g) all-purpose flour

½ cup (55 g) unsweetened cocoa powder

1 tsp iodized salt

1 tbsp (14 g) baking powder

1 tsp baking soda

1 cup (175 g) white chocolate chips (optional)

Chill the center: Place your jar of chocolate hazelnut spread in the freezer for a few hours. This will stiffen the spread so it's ready to scoop later.

For this recipe it's essential that your chocolaty center doesn't leak out of those cookies! Start by spooning about a tablespoon (15 g) of the chilled spread into a ball (I like to use a small, clamping cookie scooper) and place on a plate. Once you have formed all your center spheres, place the plate in the freezer until your dough is prepared.

Make the cookie dough: In a stand mixer fitted with the paddle attachment, or a large bowl using a handheld mixer, combine the granulated sugar, brown sugar and butter. Mix at medium-high speed until creamed, about 2 minutes. Scrape the mixture from the sides and paddle/beaters with a rubber spatula, then mix again until fully incorporated. This is complete when your mixture is light, fluffy and off-white.

Add the eggs, egg yolks, red velvet emulsion and red food coloring, then mix until just combined.

Into a separate bowl, sift together your flour, cocoa powder, salt, baking powder and baking soda, then add the flour mixture to your wet mixture in three parts, making sure to scrape the bowl before each dry addition, to clear the butter from the sides of the bowl.

If adding the white chocolate chips: Once your dough is totally combined, turn off your mixer and, using a rubber spatula, fold the white chocolate chips into the dough.

(continued)

RED VELVET CHOCOLATE HAZELNUT STUFFED COOKIES (CONTINUED)

For Rolling

1 tbsp (7 g) ground cinnamon

1 cup (200 g) granulated sugar

Preheat the oven to 375°F (190°C). Line two baking sheets with parchment paper.

For rolling: Stir together the cinnamon and granulated sugar in a shallow bowl, and set aside.

You can separate the dough into eight equal-sized balls or use a kitchen scale and weigh them all to about 6 ounces (170 g) each. Roll each portion in your cinnamon sugar mixture. Place a dough ball in your palm and push it into a bowl shape, using your fingers. Place one of the chilled chocolate hazelnut spread balls into the depression you made in the dough. Pinch the cookie dough closed around the center, rolling it into a smooth ball between your palms. Repeat to fill all the dough balls.

Place dough balls 3 inches (8 cm) apart on the prepared pans. Bake for 12 to 14 minutes, or until they reach your ideal firmness. Remove from the oven. Let them rest on the pans for about 10 minutes, then serve.

STUFFED CARROT CAKE COOKIES

Yields 7 to 8 giant cookies

Early into my TikTok baking journey, I was simultaneously sharing my recipes along with my pregnancy with Theodore. When I stepped away from giant cookies for maternity leave (mostly because my ankles had met maximum capacity), I embarked on a series of tricks to get that brat out of me. At 40 weeks and three days, I shared my favorite recipe: a moist carrot cake. I called it the "Get Out of Me Carrot Cake." Twelve hours later, Theodore Robin was here.

This recipe is my hold-in-one-hand version of a classic dessert.

Center
1 (8-oz [225-g]) package cream cheese, at room temperature

4 cups (480 g) sifted powdered sugar

2 tsp (10 ml) vanilla extract

Cookie Dough
½ cup (100 g) granulated sugar

1 cup (225 g) light brown sugar

¾ cup (1½ sticks [170 g]) noniodized salted butter, at room temperature

2 large eggs

1 large egg yolk

2 tsp (10 ml) vanilla extract

Make the center: In a medium-sized bowl, beat your cream cheese; it should become soft. Add the powdered sugar and vanilla, then continue to beat until fluffy and combined. Cover the bowl with plastic wrap and chill. To fill your cookies with the cream cheese frosting, you'll need it chilled enough to scoop.

Make the cookie dough: In a stand mixer fitted with the paddle attachment, or a large bowl using a handheld mixer, combine the granulated sugar, brown sugar and butter. Mix at medium-high speed until creamed, about 2 minutes. Scrape the mixture from the sides and paddle/beaters with a rubber spatula, then mix again until fully incorporated.

Add the eggs, egg yolk and vanilla, then mix until just combined.

(continued)

STUFFED CARROT CAKE COOKIES (CONTINUED)

4 cups (500 g) all-purpose flour

3 tbsp (24 g) cornstarch

1 tsp iodized salt

1 tsp baking powder

1 tsp baking soda

1 tsp freshly grated nutmeg

1 tsp ground ginger

1½ tsp (4 g) ground cinnamon

1 cup (110 g) shredded carrot (wring out the shreds in cheesecloth to release extra liquid)

½ cup (55 g) chopped, roasted pecans (optional)

Into a separate bowl, sift together your flour, cornstarch, salt, baking powder, baking soda, nutmeg, ginger and cinnamon, then add the flour mixture to your wet mixture in three parts, making sure to scrape the bowl before each dry addition, to clear the butter from the sides of the bowl. Add the shredded carrot and pecans (if using) and mix.

Cover your bowl with plastic wrap and chill in the refrigerator for 30 minutes, or until the dough is cold but still shapeable. While the dough is chilling, preheat the oven to 375°F (190°C). Line two baking sheets with parchment paper.

After the dough has chilled, divide it into eight balls or weigh to roughly 6 ounces (170 g) each. Using a large spoon or your fingers, press into the middle of each cookie dough ball to create a small space into which to place the cream cheese frosting. Using a tablespoon or a #100 cookie scoop, scoop a dollop of the cream cheese frosting and drop it into the depression in the cookie dough ball. Fold the surrounding cookie dough around the frosting and roll back into a ball. Repeat to fill the other dough balls. The cookies will be fairly sticky to the touch; that's normal!

Place four or five filled dough balls 3 inches (8 cm) apart on the prepared pans and lightly press on the top of each dough ball. Bake your cookies for 12 to 14 minutes, or until they have beautiful, golden-brown edges. Remove from the oven. Let them rest on the pans for 10 to 15 minutes, then serve.

COCONUT CAKE COOKIES

Baking a coconut cake for my husband for the first time is a core memory for me. It was the first birthday we celebrated together prior to our marriage, and I was dead set on making him an unforgettable cake. I made a four-layer moist coconut cake topped with buttercream, coconut macaroons and chocolate ganache. One bite and his eyes were rolling into the back of his head. Can you blame him for proposing that same year? This recipe is a combination of that cake, macaroon and ganache that led to "'I dos."

Cookie Dough

1¼ cups (281 g) light brown sugar

¾ cup (1½ sticks [170 g]) unsalted butter, at room temperature

2 large eggs

1 tbsp (15 ml) vanilla extract

¼ cup (60 ml) coconut milk

1½ cups (180 g) shredded, sweetened coconut, plus 1 cup (120 g) for rolling

3½ cups (438 g) all-purpose flour

¼ cup (32 g) cornstarch

1 tsp iodized salt

1 tsp baking powder

1 tsp baking soda

Ganache Drizzle

½ cup (88 g) semisweet chocolate chips

½ cup (120 ml) heavy cream

Make the cookie dough: In a stand mixer fitted with the paddle attachment, or a large bowl using a handheld mixer, combine the brown sugar and butter. Mix at medium-high speed until creamed, about 2 minutes. Scrape the mixture from the sides and paddle/beaters with a rubber spatula, then mix again until fully incorporated. This is complete when your mixture is light, fluffy and off-white. Add the eggs, vanilla, coconut milk and 1½ cups (180 g) of the shredded coconut, then mix until just combined.

Into a separate bowl, whisk together your flour, cornstarch, salt, baking powder and baking soda, then add the flour mixture to your wet mixture in three parts, making sure to scrape the bowl before each dry addition, to clear the butter from the sides of the bowl. Cover your bowl with plastic wrap and chill in the refrigerator for 30 minutes, or until the dough is cold but still shapeable. While the dough is chilling, preheat the oven to 375°F (190°C). Line two baking sheets with parchment paper. Place the remaining shredded coconut in a shallow bowl.

Make the ganache drizzle: Place the chocolate in a heat-safe bowl. In a small saucepan, heat the cream over medium heat until it just begins to simmer. Pour the cream over the chocolate and stir until you have a smooth ganache. Set aside.

You can separate the chilled dough into eight equal-sized balls or use a kitchen scale and weigh them all to about 6 ounces (170 g) each. Roll each dough ball in more shredded coconut. Place them 3 inches (8 cm) apart on your prepared pans and lightly press with your palm to secure them to the parchment. Bake for 12 to 14 minutes, or until they reach your ideal firmness. Remove from the oven. Let your cookies rest on the pans for 5 to 10 minutes and drizzle ganache over each cookie before serving.

TIRAMISU GIANT COOKIES

Tiramisu is one of my favorite desserts—an Italian classic made with ladyfingers, coffee and liqueur. Luckily for you, this recipe doesn't require hours of prep, a trip to Italy or a pastry degree. Just like this timeless dish, my cookie is topped with a mascarpone and cocoa topping.

Ladyfingers
8 to 10 ladyfingers

¼ cup (60 ml) instant coffee

1 tbsp (15 ml) rum

Cookie Dough
½ cup (100 g) granulated sugar

1 cup (225 g) light brown sugar

1 cup (2 sticks [227 g]) unsalted butter, at room temperature

2 large eggs

1 large egg yolk

1 tsp vanilla extract

1 tsp coffee emulsion (available from bakery supply shops or online)

1 tsp granulated instant coffee

3½ cups (438 g) all-purpose flour

1 tsp iodized salt

1 tsp baking powder

1 tsp baking soda

Soak the ladyfingers: Place the ladyfingers in a shallow dish. In a small bowl or measuring cup, mix together the instant coffee and rum and pour over the ladyfingers. Let soak while you prepare your dough.

Make the cookie dough: In a stand mixer fitted with the paddle attachment, or a large bowl using a handheld mixer, combine the granulated sugar, brown sugar and butter. Mix at medium-high speed until creamed, about 2 minutes. Scrape the mixture from the sides and paddle/beaters with a rubber spatula, then mix again until fully incorporated. This is complete when your mixture is light, fluffy and off-white.

Add the eggs, egg yolk, vanilla, coffee emulsion and instant coffee, then mix until just combined.

Into a separate bowl, sift together your flour, salt, baking powder and baking soda, then add the flour mixture to your wet mixture in three parts, making sure to scrape the bowl before each dry addition, to clear the butter from the sides of the bowl. Once your dough is fully combined, add your soaked ladyfingers and gently fold in; they should fall apart into your mixture.

Cover your bowl with plastic wrap and chill in the refrigerator for 30 minutes, or until the dough is cold but still shapeable. While the dough is chilling, preheat the oven to 375°F (190°C). Line two baking sheets with parchment paper.

You can separate the chilled dough into eight equal-sized balls or use a kitchen scale and weigh them all to about 6 ounces (170 g) each. Place 3 inches (8 cm) apart on the prepared pans and bake for 10 to 12 minutes, or until they reach your ideal firmness.

Topping
2 large egg yolks

¼ cup (50 g) granulated sugar

⅓ cup (80 ml) heavy cream

½ cup (120 g) mascarpone

For Dusting
Unsweetened cocoa powder, for dusting

While your cookies are baking, make your topping: In a medium-sized bowl, beat together your egg yolks and granulated sugar until fluffy. Add the cream and mascarpone, then beat until the mixture has a smooth consistency.

Once your cookies are baked, remove from the oven and let them rest on the pans until they are cool to the touch. Using an offset spatula or a piping bag, spread the topping on each cookie. Finally, dust each cookie with cocoa.

CHAPTER 3:
FAMILY
HEIRLOOMS

All of the cookies you'll find in this book are full of flavor and fun, but they also represent the memories that inspired me. I grew up with a single mom and a small extended family. The few recipes that were passed down, I held on to very dearly and worked into my giant cookies.

On days when I am hit the hardest with the grief of losing my mom, Jenny Wren, I remember how much she adored the smell of lavender and my lemon cookies. When Christmas sneaks up on me, I look forward to the first gingersnap of the season. The recipes in this chapter represent some of the people I love most in the world and memories I hold dearest.

THE JENNY WREN

Developing this cookie brought up so many emotions. My mother, Jenny Wren, fought brain cancer for 11 years. Even on the days she couldn't bear to eat, she would always eat a cookie I made. Each time I make this cookie, I'm reminded of her best days, sitting on the back porch of my grandparent's mountain-facing Virginia home in mid-summer enjoying a lavender lemon cookie.

Cookie Dough

1½ cups (300 g) granulated sugar

Zest of 2 lemons

2 tsp (6 g) food-safe lavender buds

¾ cup (1½ sticks [170 g]) unsalted butter, at room temperature

2 large eggs

1 large egg yolk

2 tsp (10 ml) lemon emulsion (available from bakery supply shops or online)

4 cups (500 g) all-purpose flour

¼ cup (32 g) cornstarch

1 tsp iodized salt

1 tsp baking powder

1 tsp baking soda

For Rolling

½ cup (100 g) granulated sugar

½ cup (60 g) powdered sugar

1 tsp (3 g) food-safe lavender buds

Make the cookie dough: In a food processor, blend together your granulated sugar, lemon zest and lavender buds until fragrant.

In a stand mixer fitted with the paddle attachment, or a large bowl using a handheld mixer, combine the sugar mixture and butter and beat at medium-high speed until light and fluffy, about 2 minutes. Scrape the mixture from the sides and paddle/beaters with a rubber spatula, then mix again until fully incorporated.

Add the eggs, egg yolk and lemon emulsion, then mix until just combined. Into a separate bowl, sift together your flour, corn-starch, salt, baking powder and baking soda, then add the flour mixture to your wet mixture in three parts. Make sure to scrape the bowl before each dry addition, to clear your wet ingredients from the sides of the bowl.

Cover your bowl with plastic wrap and chill in the refrigerator for 30 minutes, or until the dough is cold but still shapeable. While the dough is chilling, preheat the oven to 375°F (190°C) and line two baking sheets with parchment paper.

Make your rolling mixture: Place your granulated sugar, powdered sugar and lavender buds in the food processor and blend until the lavender buds are smaller and fragrant. Transfer to a shallow bowl.

You can separate the chilled dough into eight equal-sized balls or use a kitchen scale and weigh them all to about 6 ounces (170 g) each.

Roll each cookie in the lavender sugar and then flatten them a bit. Place them 3 inches (8 cm) apart on the prepared pans. Bake for 12 to 14 minutes, or until they reach your ideal firmness. Remove from the oven. Let your cookies rest on the pans for about 10 minutes before digging in.

GIANT GINGERSNAP

There are a few flavors that I strongly associate with Christmas: molasses, cinnamon, peppermint, and most importantly, ginger. The first Christmas cookie I ever baked, a favorite of my mother's, was the classic gingersnap. This recipe is my holiday favorite turned bigger and chewier than ever.

Cookie Dough

1½ cups (300 g) granulated sugar

¾ cup (1½ sticks [170 g]) unsalted butter, at room temperature

2 large eggs

1 large egg yolk

¼ cup (60 ml) molasses

3½ cups (438 g) all-purpose flour

¼ cup (32 g) cornstarch

1 tsp iodized salt

1 tsp baking powder

1 tsp baking soda

2 tsp (5 g) ground cinnamon

1 tbsp (6 g) ground ginger

For Rolling

1 cup (200 g) turbinado sugar

In a stand mixer fitted with the paddle attachment, or a large bowl using a handheld mixer, combine the granulated sugar and butter. Mix at medium-high speed until creamed, about 2 minutes. Scrape the mixture from the sides and paddle/beaters with a rubber spatula, then mix until fully incorporated. This is complete when your mixture is light, fluffy and off-white.

Add the eggs, egg yolk and molasses, then mix until just combined.

Into a separate bowl, sift together your flour, corn-starch, salt, baking powder, baking soda, cinnamon and ginger, and add the flour mixture to your wet mixture in three parts, making sure to scrape the bowl before each dry addition, to clear the butter from the sides of the bowl.

Cover your bowl with plastic wrap and chill in the refrigerator for 30 minutes, or until the dough is cold but still shapeable. While the dough is chilling, preheat the oven to 375°F (190°C). Line two baking sheets with parchment paper. Place the turbinado sugar in a shallow bowl.

You can separate the chilled dough into eight equal-sized balls or use a kitchen scale and weigh them all to about 6 ounces (170 g) each. Roll in the turbinado sugar and place 3 inches (8 cm) apart on the prepared pans. I like to give each cookie a gentle push with my palm so they're secured to the parchment. Bake for 12 to 14 minutes, or until they reach your ideal firmness. Remove from the oven. Let your cookies rest on the pans for 5 to 10 minutes, then serve.

GIANT SUGAR COOKIES WITH BUTTERCREAM

Yields 8 giant cookies

Buttercream is one of the most versatile toppings for a cookie. With a few additions of any kind of extract, zest, caramels or color, you can transform a simple, fluffy sugar cookie into a vessel of flavor.

Cookie Dough

1½ cups (300 g) granulated sugar

¾ cup (1½ sticks [170 g]) unsalted butter, at room temperature

2 large eggs

2 large egg yolks

2 tsp (10 ml) vanilla extract

4 cups (500 g) all-purpose flour

¼ cup (32 g) cornstarch

2 tsp (12 g) iodized salt

2 tsp (9 g) baking powder

2 tsp (9 g) baking soda

For Rolling

1 cup (200 g) granulated sugar

Buttercream

1 cup (2 sticks [227 g]) unsalted butter, at room temperature

4 to 6 cups (480 to 720 g) powdered sugar

¼ tsp salt

2 tsp (10 ml) vanilla or almond extract

1 tbsp (15 ml) heavy cream, or as needed

Pink gel food coloring (optional)

Make the cookie dough: In a stand mixer fitted with the paddle attachment, or a large bowl using a handheld mixer, combine the granulated sugar and butter. Mix at medium-high speed until creamed, about 2 minutes. Scrape the mixture from the sides and paddle/beaters with a rubber spatula, then mix until fully incorporated. Add the eggs, egg yolks and vanilla, then mix until just combined.

Into a separate bowl, sift together your flour, cornstarch, salt, baking powder and baking soda and add the flour mixture to your wet mixture in three parts, making sure to scrape the bowl before each dry addition, to clear the butter from the sides of the bowl. Cover your bowl with plastic wrap and chill in the refrigerator for 30 minutes, or until the dough is cold but still shapeable. While the dough is chilling, preheat the oven to 375°F (190°C). Line two baking sheets with parchment paper. Place the granulated sugar for rolling in a shallow bowl.

Make the buttercream: In a stand mixer fitted with the paddle attachment, or a large bowl using a handheld mixer, add the butter, powdered sugar and salt. Mix on low speed until mostly incorporated. Add the vanilla, increase the speed to medium-high and mix until smooth. Adjust the consistency with heavy cream as desired. If you're using pink gel food coloring, add it now. Beat the buttercream on high speed for 8 to 9 minutes.

Bake the cookies: You can separate the chilled dough into eight equal-sized balls or use a kitchen scale and weigh them all to about 6 ounces (170 g) each. Roll each ball in the granulated sugar. Place 3 inches (8 cm) apart on the prepared pans. Bake for 10 to 12 minutes, or until they reach your ideal firmness. Once the cookies are completely cooled, use a butterknife or offset spatula to spread a generous amount of buttercream on top of each cookie.

JUMBO GOOEY BUTTER COOKIES

Yields
8 giant
cookies

One of the greatest things to come of my mother moving us to the South was my introduction to a little something called "gooey butter cake." In Tennessee, everyone's grandma has her own favorite version, but they all come down to the same essential ingredients: yellow cake mix, cream cheese and vanilla. If you aren't a fan of a generous bite of cream cheese, skip the stuffing.

Cookie Dough
½ cup (100 g) granulated sugar

¾ cup (1½ sticks [170 g]) unsalted butter, at room temperature

2 large eggs

1 large egg yolk

2 tsp (10 ml) vanilla extract

2 (15-oz [425-g]) boxes yellow cake mix

½ cup (60 g) all-purpose flour

¼ cup (32 g) cornstarch

Center
1 (8-oz [225-g]) package cream cheese, chilled and cut into 1-oz (28-g) cubes

For Rolling
1 cup (120 g) sifted powdered sugar

Make the cookie dough: In a stand mixer fitted with the paddle attachment, or a large bowl using a handheld mixer, combine the granulated sugar and butter. Mix at medium-high speed until creamed, about 2 minutes. Scrape the mixture from the sides and paddle/beaters with a rubber spatula, then mix until fully incorporated.

Add the eggs, egg yolk and vanilla, then mix until just combined.

Into a separate bowl, sift together your cake mix, flour and cornstarch, then add this dry mixture to your wet mixture in three parts. Make sure to scrape the bowl before each dry addition to clear your wet ingredients, from the sides of the bowl.

Cover your bowl with plastic wrap and chill in the refrigerator for 30 minutes, or until the dough is cold but still shapeable. While the dough is chilling, preheat the oven to 375°F (190°C) and line two baking sheets with parchment paper.

Add the center: You can separate the chilled dough into eight equal-sized balls or use a kitchen scale and weigh them all to about 6 ounces (170 g) each. Using a large spoon or your fingers, press into the middle of each dough ball to create a small space in which to place one cube of chilled cream cheese. Then, fold the surrounding cookie dough around the cream cheese and roll back into a ball. Place the sifted powdered sugar in a shallow bowl and roll each ball in the sugar.

Place four or five filled dough balls 3 inches (8 cm) apart on the prepared pans and lightly press on the tops of each dough ball. Bake your cookies for 12 to 14 minutes, or until they are golden at the edges. Remove from the oven. Let them rest on the pans for 10 to 15 minutes, then serve.

THE ELVIS

Yields 7 to 8 giant cookies

My giant cookie journey began in our beloved city of Memphis, so it's only fitting I include a giant cookie inspired by the king of rock and roll, Elvis Presley. This is a giant banana cream pie cookie with white chocolate chips and a peanut butter center.

Center
1 cup (256 g) creamy peanut butter

Cookie Dough
½ cup (100 g) granulated sugar

1 cup (225 g) light brown sugar

¾ cup (1½ sticks [170 g]) unsalted butter, at room temperature

2 large eggs

1 large egg yolk

2 tsp (10 ml) banana extract

2 tbsp (20 g) dry banana pudding mix

4 cups (500 g) all-purpose flour

3 tbsp (24 g) cornstarch

1 tsp iodized salt

1 tsp baking powder

1 tsp baking soda

1 cup (175 g) white chocolate chips

Chill the center: Fill eight 1-ounce (29-ml) wells of a silicone mold with peanut butter and freeze. Keep frozen until you're ready to fill your cookies.

Make the cookie dough: In a stand mixer fitted with the paddle attachment, or a large bowl using a handheld mixer, combine the granulated sugar, brown sugar and butter and mix on medium-high speed until light and fluffy, about 2 minutes. Scrape the mixture from the sides and paddle/beaters with a rubber spatula, then mix until fully incorporated. Add the eggs and egg yolk, banana extract and pudding mix, then mix until combined.

Into a separate bowl, sift together your flour, cornstarch, salt, baking powder and baking soda, and add the flour mixture to your wet mixture in three parts, making sure to scrape the bowl before each dry addition, to clear the butter from the sides of the bowl. Turn off the mixer and, using a rubber spatula, fold in the white chocolate chips.

Cover your bowl with plastic wrap and chill in the refrigerator for 30 minutes, or until the dough is cold but still shapeable. While the dough is chilling, preheat the oven to 375°F (190°C). Line two baking sheets with parchment paper.

Add the center: You can separate the chilled dough into eight equal-sized balls or use a kitchen scale and weigh them all to about 6 ounces (170 g) each. Using a large spoon or your fingers, press into the middle of each cookie dough ball to create a small space into which to place your frozen peanut butter. Then, fold the surrounding cookie dough around the peanut butter and roll back into a ball.

Place four or five filled dough balls 3 inches (8 cm) apart on the prepared pans and lightly press on the tops of each dough ball. Bake your cookies for 12 to 14 minutes, or until they are firm and set. Remove from the oven. Let them rest on the pans for 10 to 15 minutes before digging in.

DADDY'S NO-BAKE COOKIES

Yields 5 to 6 giant cookies

If there's one thing my husband can do better than me, it's bake biscuits. Oh and make no-bake cookies. These were in constant demand during my one thousand years of being pregnant (yes, it was nine months, but ask anyone who's been pregnant, and they'll agree on the timeline). Peanut butter, chocolate, oats and hardly any work come together for a delicious result.

1 cup (2 sticks [227 g]) unsalted butter, at room temperature

3 cups (600 g) granulated sugar

1 cup (240 ml) milk

4 cups (320 g) quick oats

1 cup (110 g) unsweetened cocoa powder

1 tbsp (15 ml) vanilla extract

1 cup (256 g) peanut butter

In a medium-sized saucepan over medium heat, bring the butter, sugar and milk to a boil. Lower the heat to low and let simmer for 3 to 5 minutes. Add the oats, cocoa powder, vanilla and peanut butter, and stir over low heat until thoroughly combined.

Remove your pan from the heat and set aside to cool.

Once your mixture is cool to the touch, begin forming your cookies. With lightly greased hands, scoop about a half cup (115 g) of your mixture and form it into a large, round cookie shape. Place on a wax paper—lined cookie sheet. Repeat this until all of your mixture is shaped into cookies and chill. I prefer to pop mine in the freezer so they're nice and cold before serving.

PFEFFERNÜSSE

Yields
8 giant
cookies

If any food on the planet could be described as "smells like Christmas," it would be the traditional Pfeffernüsse. This is a festive five-spice cookie served to my family at Christmas time. The holidays with my family wouldn't be complete without this sugar-dusted holiday delight.

Cookie Dough
1½ cups (300 g) granulated sugar

1 cup (2 sticks [227 g]) unsalted butter, at room temperature

2 large eggs

2 large egg yolks

1 cup (240 ml) honey

4 cups (500 g) all-purpose flour

¼ cup (32 g) cornstarch

1 tsp iodized salt

1 tsp baking powder

1 tsp baking soda

2 tsp (5 g) ground cinnamon

2 tsp (4 g) ground cardamom

2 tsp (5 g) ground aniseed

2 tsp (4 g) ground allspice

2 tsp (4 g) ground cloves

2 tsp (4 g) freshly ground black pepper

For Rolling
2 cups (240 g) sifted powdered sugar

In a stand mixer fitted with the paddle attachment, or a large bowl using a handheld mixer, combine the granulated sugar and butter. Mix at medium-high speed until creamed, about 2 minutes. Scrape the mixture from the sides and paddle/beaters with a rubber spatula, then mix until fully incorporated. This is complete when your mixture is light, fluffy and off-white.

Add the eggs, egg yolks and honey, then mix until just combined.

Into a separate bowl, sift together your flour, cornstarch, salt, baking powder, baking soda, cinnamon, cardamom, aniseed, allspice, cloves and pepper. Add the flour mixture to your wet mixture in three parts, making sure to scrape the bowl before each dry addition, to clear your wet ingredients from the sides of the bowl.

Cover your bowl with plastic wrap and chill in the refrigerator for 20 minutes, or until the dough is cold but still shapeable. While the dough is chilling, preheat the oven to 375°F (190°C) and line two baking sheets with parchment paper.

You can separate the chilled dough into eight equal-sized balls or use a kitchen scale and weigh them all to about 6 ounces (170 g) each. Place 3 inches (8 cm) apart on the prepared pans. Bake for 12 to 14 minutes, or until they reach your ideal firmness. Once the cookies have cooled on the pans, place the powdered sugar in a shallow bowl and roll each cookie in the sugar. They're ready to eat!

THE TEDDY BEAR

Yields 8 giant cookies

This cookie is named for our curly-haired, sharp-toothed cherub child, Theodore. Cinnamon, sugar and a heaping serving of Teddy Grahams™.

½ cup (100 g) granulated sugar

1 cup (225 g) light brown sugar

½ cup (1 stick [114 g]) unsalted butter, at room temperature

2 large eggs

2 large egg yolks

2 tsp (10 ml) vanilla extract

4 cups (500 g) all-purpose flour

3 tbsp (24 g) cornstarch

1 tsp iodized salt

1 tsp baking powder

1 tsp baking soda

1 tsp ground cinnamon

½ cup (30 g) crushed honey grahams, such as Teddy Grahams, plus more for rolling

In a stand mixer fitted with the paddle attachment, or a large bowl using a handheld mixer, combine the granulated sugar, brown sugar and butter. Mix at medium-high speed until creamed, about 2 minutes. Scrape the mixture from the sides and paddle/beaters with a rubber spatula, then mix until fully incorporated. Add the eggs, egg yolks and vanilla, then mix until just combined.

Into a separate bowl, sift together your flour, cornstarch, salt, baking powder, baking soda and cinnamon, then add the flour mixture to your wet mixture in three parts, making sure to scrape the bowl before each dry addition, to clear the butter from the sides of the bowl. Turn off the mixer and, with a rubber spatula, fold ½ cup (30 g) of the crushed grahams into the dough.

Cover your bowl with plastic wrap and chill in the refrigerator for 30 minutes, or until the dough is cold but still shapeable. While the dough is chilling, preheat the oven to 375°F (190°C). Line two baking sheets with parchment paper.

Using your kitchen scale, form the chilled dough into balls anywhere from 6.5 to 6.8 ounces (184 to 193 g), or divide it into eight equal-sized balls. Press extra crushed graham crackers onto the top of each ball or roll the balls in the crushed grahams.

Place four or five balls 3 inches (8 cm) apart on the prepared pans and lightly press on the tops of each dough ball. Bake your cookies for 12 to 14 minutes, or until they have beautiful, golden-brown edges. Remove from the oven. Let them rest on the pans for 10 to 15 minutes, to prevent them from falling apart.

CHAPTER 4:
BITS &
PIECES

All the giant cookies I've ever made have always started with the same question: "What can I possibly shove into this cookie to make it even better?"

Crushed chocolate sandwich cookies, iodized salted caramels, potato chips, white chocolate, pretzels—anything you can think of, I've stuffed and crushed into a giant cookie. These recipes are my favorite "what ifs" turned into such delicious combinations as Fruity Pebbles™ with marshmallow (page 74) and bourbon, bacon and maple syrup (page 66). If the question is "Can it cookie?" the answer is yes. It absolutely can.

COOKIES 'N' DREAM

Yields 7 to 8 giant cookies

This was one of the first items to be launched on my original giant cookie menu. Those familiar store-bought chocolate sandwich cookies aren't just one of the world's best, dunkable cookies; they're also one of the best ingredients thrown into other treats. I top my giant cookie off with a decent amount of white chocolate and—BOOM!— you've got a giant melty cookies-and-cream treat of your . . . dreams. Get it?

¾ cup (150 g) granulated sugar

½ cup (115 g) light brown sugar

½ cup (1 stick [114 g]) unsalted butter, at room temperature

2 large eggs

2 large egg yolks

1 tsp vanilla extract

3½ cups (438 g) all-purpose flour

¼ cup (32 g) cornstarch

½ tsp iodized salt

½ tsp baking powder

½ tsp baking soda

12 whole chocolate sandwich cookies (I use Oreos™), filling included, crushed

1½ cups (263 g) white chocolate chips

For Rolling
1 cup (200 g) granulated sugar

1 tbsp (7 g) ground cinnamon

In a stand mixer fitted with the paddle attachment, or a large bowl using a handheld mixer, combine the granulated sugar, brown sugar and butter. Mix at medium-high speed until light and fluffy, about 2 minutes. Scrape the mixture from the sides and paddle/beaters with a rubber spatula, then mix until fully incorporated. This is complete when your mixture is light, fluffy and off-white.

Add the eggs, egg yolks and vanilla, then mix until just combined.

Into a separate bowl, sift together your flour, cornstarch, salt, baking powder and baking soda and add the flour mixture to your wet mixture in three parts, making sure to scrape the bowl before each dry addition to clear the butter from the sides of the bowl. Pour in your crushed cookies and white chocolate chips and continue to mix until fully incorporated.

Cover your bowl with plastic wrap and chill in the refrigerator for 30 minutes, or until the dough is cold but still shapeable. While the dough is chilling, preheat the oven to 375°F (190°C). Line two baking sheets with parchment paper. To make the cinnamon sugar for rolling, stir together the granulated sugar and cinnamon in a shallow bowl.

You can separate the chilled dough into eight equal-sized balls or use a kitchen scale and weigh them all to about 6 ounces (170 g) each. Roll each cookie in your cinnamon sugar mixture. Place 3 inches (8 cm) apart on the prepared pans and bake for 10 to 12 minutes, or until they reach your ideal firmness. Remove from the oven. Let them rest for about 10 minutes before lifting from the pans.

GIANT CARAMEL STUFFED PECAN CHOCOLATE CHIP COOKIES

Yields 7 to 8 giant cookies

Once upon a time . . . a gourmet iodized salted caramel candymaker from our hometown of Memphis asked BluffCakes to collaborate and—BOOM!—one of our most popular and raved-about cookies was born: a classic giant chocolate chip cookie packed with roasted pecans and filled with a gooey salted caramel center. Pull them straight from the oven and break open for a mouthwatering caramel stretch hidden inside.

½ cup (100 g) granulated sugar

1 cup (225 g) light brown sugar

½ cup (1 stick [114 g]) unsalted butter, at room temperature

2 large eggs

2 large egg yolks

4 cups (500 g) all-purpose flour

3 tbsp (24 g) cornstarch

1 tsp iodized salt

1 tsp baking powder

1 tsp baking soda

1 cup (175 g) semisweet chocolate chips

1 cup (110 g) finely chopped roasted and iodized salted pecans

7 oz (198 g) Iodized salted caramels (I prefer Shotwell Candy Co. brand)

In a stand mixer fitted with the paddle attachment, or a large bowl using a handheld mixer, combine the granulated sugar, brown sugar and butter. Mix at medium-high speed until creamed, about 2 minutes. Scrape the mixture from the sides and paddle/beaters with a rubber spatula, then mix until fully incorporated. This is complete when your mixture is light, fluffy and off-white.

Add the eggs and egg yolks, then mix until just combined.

Into a separate bowl, sift together your flour, corn-starch, salt, baking powder and baking soda, then add the flour mixture to your wet mixture in three parts, making sure to scrape the bowl before each dry addition, to clear the butter from the sides of the bowl.

Turn off the mixer and, using a rubber spatula, fold the chocolate chips and pecans into the dough.

(continued)

GIANT CARAMEL STUFFED PECAN CHOCOLATE CHIP COOKIES (CONTINUED)

Cover your bowl with plastic wrap and chill in the refrigerator for 30 minutes, or until the dough is cold but still shapeable. While the dough is chilling, preheat the oven to 375°F (190°C). Line two baking sheets with parchment paper.

Using your kitchen scale, form the chilled dough into balls anywhere from 6.5 to 6.8 ounces (184 to 193 g), or divide it into eight equal-sized balls.

Using a large spoon or your fingers, press into the middle of each cookie dough ball to create a small space into which to place one or two caramels. Then, fold the surrounding cookie dough around the caramel(s) and roll back into a ball.

Place four or five filled dough balls 3 inches (8 cm) apart on the prepared pans and lightly press on the tops of each dough ball. Bake your cookies for 12 to 14 minutes, or until they have beautiful, golden-brown edges. Remove from the oven. Let them rest on the pans for 10 to 15 minutes to prevent them from falling apart.

BROWNIE-STUFFED COWBOY COOKIES

Yields 7 to 8 giant cookies

This coconut, chocolate chip and pecan cowboy cookie is hiding a fudgy secret—a thick brownie center.

Brownies for Stuffing

1 cup (2 sticks [227 g]) unsalted butter, plus more for cake pan

2 cups (400 g) granulated sugar

1 cup (110 g) unsweetened cocoa powder, plus more for cake pan

4 large eggs, beaten

1½ tbsp (23 g) vanilla extract

⅔ cup (83 g) all-purpose flour

Cookie Dough

1 cup (225 g) light brown sugar

½ cup (100 g) granulated sugar

¾ cup (1½ sticks [170 g]) unsalted butter, at room temperature

2 large eggs

2 large egg yolks

2 tsp (10 ml) vanilla extract

Make the brownies: Preheat the oven to 350°F (180°C).

In a small saucepan, melt the butter over medium heat. Once it is melted, add the sugar and 1 cup (110 g) of cocoa powder, and stir over medium heat until smooth. Remove from the heat and set aside until the mixture is warm to the touch, but not hot.

Gently whisk in the eggs and vanilla. Add the flour and continue to whisk until the batter is smooth.

Line an 8-inch square (20-cm) cake pan with parchment paper, generously butter, then dust with cocoa on all sides. Pour batter into the prepared pan and bake for 30 to 40 minutes, or until the center is set. Remove from the oven, let cool, then place in the freezer to chill.

Make the cookie dough: In a stand mixer fitted with the paddle attachment, or a large bowl using a handheld mixer, combine the brown sugar, granulated sugar and butter, and beat together at medium-high speed for about 2 minutes. Scrape the mixture from the sides and paddle with a rubber spatula and mix until lighter in color and fluffy.

Add the eggs, egg yolks and vanilla, and mix until just combined.

(continued)

BROWNIE-STUFFED COWBOY COOKIES (CONTINUED)

3½ cups (438 g) flour

3 tbsp (24 g) cornstarch

1 tsp salt

1 tsp baking powder

1 tsp baking soda

2 tsp (5 g) ground cinnamon

1½ cups (125 g) unsweetened shredded coconut

1 cup (175 g) semisweet chocolate chips

1 cup (110 g) chopped, roasted pecans

In a separate bowl, whisk together your flour, corn-starch, salt, baking powder, baking soda, cinnamon and coconut, then add the flour mixture to the butter mixture in three parts. Make sure to scrape the bowl before each dry addition, to clear butter from the sides of the mixer.

Once your wet and dry ingredients are combined, fold the chocolate chips and pecans into the dough with a rubber spatula.

Cover your bowl with plastic wrap and chill in the refrigerator for 30 minutes, or until the dough is cold but still shapeable. While the dough is chilling, preheat the oven to 375°F (190°C) and cut your chilled brownies into 1-inch (2.5-cm) squares.

Line two cookie sheets with parchment paper. Using your scale, weigh the chilled dough into balls to roughly 6 ounces (170 g), or divide the dough into eight equal-sized balls. Place a dough ball in your palm and push it into a bowl shape with your fingers. Tuck a brownie into the center of the cookie and pinch the cookie dough closed around the brownie, rolling the dough smooth between your palms. Repeat with the remaining dough balls and brownie squares.

Place the cookies 3 inches (8 cm) apart on the prepared pans, giving them each a light push to secure them to the parchment. Bake for 12 to 15 minutes, or until they reach your ideal firmness. Let them rest on the pans for about 10 minutes, then serve.

GIANT UBE COOKIES

I first encountered ube in the most unique form from a Memphis local Filipino spot—an ube cake roll that I tasted in my dreams for weeks. At first sight, ube may look like just some purple yam, but it has a distinct nutty vanilla flavor I've grown to crave. This cookie is completed with a sifted sugar crinkle finish to make these extra special.

Cookie Dough

¾ cup (150 g) granulated sugar

¾ cup (169 g) light brown sugar

¾ cup (1½ sticks [170 g]) unsalted butter, at room temperature

2 large eggs

2 large egg yolks

1 tbsp (15 ml) ube extract

⅓ cup (75 g) ube jam

3½ cups (438 g) all-purpose flour

¼ cup (32 g) cornstarch

1 tsp iodized salt

1 tsp baking powder

1 tsp baking soda

For Rolling

1 cup (120 g) sifted powdered sugar

In a stand mixer fitted with the paddle attachment, or a large bowl using a handheld mixer, combine the granulated sugar, brown sugar and butter. Mix at medium-high speed until creamed, about 2 minutes. Scrape the mixture from the sides and paddle/beaters with a rubber spatula, then mix until fully incorporated. This is complete when your mixture is light, fluffy and off-white.

Add the eggs, egg yolks, ube extract and jam, then mix until just combined.

Into a separate bowl, sift together your flour, cornstarch, salt, baking powder and baking soda, then add the flour mixture to your wet mixture in three parts, making sure to scrape the bowl before each dry addition to clear your wet ingredients from the sides of the bowl.

Cover your bowl with plastic wrap and chill in the refrigerator for 20 minutes, or until the dough is cold but still shapeable. While the dough is chilling, preheat the oven to 375°F (190°C) and line two baking sheets with parchment paper. Place the powdered sugar in a shallow bowl.

You can separate the chilled dough into eight equal-sized balls or use a kitchen scale and weigh them all to about 6 ounces (170 g) each. Roll them in the powdered sugar. Place 3 inches (8 cm) apart on the prepared pans. Bake for 12 to 14 minutes, or until they reach your ideal firmness. Remove from the oven. Let your cookies rest on the pans for about 10 minutes before serving.

THE KITCHEN SINK COOKIES

This recipe should be made for any skeptic in your life who claims not to like salty-sweet combinations: a brown sugar–based cookie dough with pretzel pieces, chocolate chips and potato chips. Truthfully, when I told my husband I was going to create this cookie, he said, "Well, that's . . . interesting." But the results definitely made him literally "eat" his skepticism.

1½ cups (338 g) light brown sugar

¾ cup (1½ sticks [170 g]) unsalted butter, at room temperature

2 large eggs

2 large egg yolks

1 tsp vanilla extract

3½ cups (438 g) all-purpose flour

¼ cup (32 g) cornstarch

1 tsp iodized salt

1 tsp baking powder

1 tsp baking soda

½ cup (88 g) semisweet chocolate chips

½ cup (21 g) crushed ruffled potato chips

½ cup (50 g) crushed pretzels

In a stand mixer fitted with the paddle attachment, or a large bowl using a handheld mixer, combine the brown sugar and butter. Mix at medium-high speed until creamed, about 2 minutes. Scrape the mixture from the sides and paddle/beaters with a rubber spatula and mix until fully incorporated. This is complete when your mixture is light, fluffy and off-white.

Add the eggs, egg yolks and vanilla, then mix until just combined.

Into a separate bowl, sift together your flour, corn-starch, salt, baking powder and baking soda, then add the flour mixture to your wet mixture in three parts, making sure to scrape the bowl before each dry addition, to clear your wet ingredients from the sides of the bowl.

Turn off the mixer and, using a rubber spatula, fold the chocolate chips, potato chips and pretzels in by hand. This will ensure your "snack bits" stay nice and chunky instead of crumbled within the dough.

Cover your bowl with plastic wrap and chill in the refrigerator for 20 minutes, or until the dough is cold but still shapeable. While the dough is chilling, preheat the oven to 375°F (190°C) and line two sheets with parcment paper.

You can separate the chilled dough into eight equal-sized balls or use a kitchen scale and weigh them all to about 6 ounces (170 g) each. Place 3 inches (8 cm) apart on the prepared pans. Bake for 12 to 14 minutes, or until they reach your ideal firmness. Remove from the oven. Let your cookies rest on the pans for about 10 minutes, then serve.

MAPLE BACON PECAN GIANT COOKIES

Yields 7 to 8 giant cookies

Every Father's Day, I wake up early, pack up the children and let Cookie Daddy (or Tyler, as he's formally known) sleep in while we sneak off to get the freshest donuts from our favorite local sugar pusher—Howard's Donuts. There you'll find some of the most incredible flavors packed into warm, fluffy donuts. Each year, one donut is the star of the show: the maple bacon. It's the first one we all reach for and the inspiration behind this recipe. The perfect balance of iodized pecans, sugar and my maple bourbon glaze on top really bring it all together.

Cookie Dough

½ cup (100 g) granulated sugar

1 cup (225 g) light brown sugar

1 cup (2 sticks [227 g]) unsalted butter, at room temperature

2 large eggs

2 large egg yolks

4 cups (500 g) all-purpose flour

3 tbsp (24 g) cornstarch

1 tsp iodized salt

1 tsp baking powder

1 tsp baking soda

6 to 8 strips bacon, cooked until crispy, then chopped

½ cup (55 g) finely chopped roasted and iodized salted pecans (optional)

Maple Bourbon Glaze

¼ cup (60 ml) pure maple syrup

1½ cups (180 g) sifted powdered sugar

2 tsp (10 ml) bourbon

Make the cookie dough: In a stand mixer fitted with the paddle attachment, or a large bowl using a handheld mixer, combine the granulated sugar, brown sugar and butter. Mix at medium-high speed until creamed, about 2 minutes. Scrape the mixture from the sides and paddle/beaters with a rubber spatula and mix until fully incorporated. This is complete when your mixture is light, fluffy and off-white.

Add the eggs and egg yolks, then mix until just combined.

Into a separate bowl, sift together your flour, corn-starch, salt, baking powder and baking soda, and then add the flour mixture to your wet mixture in three parts, making sure to scrape the bowl before each dry addition, to clear the butter from the sides of the bowl.

Turn off the mixer and, using a rubber spatula, fold the bacon and pecans (if using) into the dough.

Cover your bowl with plastic wrap and chill in the refrigerator for 30 minutes, or until the dough is cold but still shapeable. While the dough is chilling, preheat the oven to 375°F (190°C). Line two baking sheets with parchment paper.

Make the glaze: In a medium-sized bowl, whisk together the maple syrup, powdered sugar and bourbon. Set aside.

You can separate the chilled dough into eight equal-sized balls or use a kitchen scale and weigh them all to about 6 ounces (170 g) each.

Place four or five balls 3 inches (8 cm) apart on the prepared pans and lightly press on the tops of each dough ball. Bake your cookies for 12 to 14 minutes, or until they have beautiful, golden-brown edges. Remove from the oven. Let them rest on the pans for 10 to 15 minutes before drizzling the glaze across each cookie and serving.

EDIBLE COOKIE DOUGH

Yields about four 1-cup (115-g) servings

I'd be lying if I said I've never snatched a taste of the cookie dough I've spent so much of my life developing. In fact (if legally allowed), I'd even encourage it. It's almost the fact you're "not supposed to eat cookie dough" that makes it even more delicious. But never fear; this recipe is completely safe and customizable no matter what you want to mix into it. This recipe is perfect for an indulgent midnight snack.

2 cups (250 g) all-purpose flour

½ cup (1 stick [114 g]) unsalted butter, at room temperature, slightly melted (soft)

1 tsp vanilla (or your choice) extract

½ cup (100 g) granulated sugar

½ cup (115 g) light brown sugar

1 cup (175 g) mini semisweet chocolate chips

2 tsp (12 g) flaky iodized salt

In a microwave-safe glass bowl, microwave your flour for 60 to 120 seconds, or until it reaches a temperature of 165°F (73°C). Spread it out on a clean cookie sheet and let cool.

In a large bowl, mix together the slightly melted butter, vanilla, granulated sugar and brown sugar. Slowly whisk in the microwaved flour until fully mixed. Pour in the chocolate chips and flaky salt and fold in with a rubber spatula.

Cover your edible dough with plastic wrap and chill for 1 to 2 hours. Serve and enjoy!

CRÈME BRÛLÉE COOKIES

Yields 7 to 8 giant cookies

Crème brûlée is a simple but elegant dessert made even better when topping off a giant cookie. The soft sugar cookie base adds another layer of indulgence with a hint of vanilla bean paste and a crisp brûlée burnt on the top.

Topping

4 ounces (113 g) cream cheese, at room temperature

½ cup (115 g) light brown sugar

½ cup (60 g) powdered sugar

2 tsp (10 ml) vanilla extract

¼ cup (50 g) granulated sugar, for caramelizing

Cookie Dough

1½ cups (300 g) granulated sugar

1 cup (2 sticks [227 g]) unsalted butter, at room temperature

2 large eggs

2 large egg yolks

1 tsp vanilla bean paste

3½ cups (438 g) all-purpose flour

1 tbsp (8 g) cornstarch

1 tsp iodized salt

1 tbsp (14 g) baking powder

1 tsp baking soda

Make the topping: In a stand mixer fitted with the paddle attachment, or a medium-sized bowl using a handheld mixer, combine the cream cheese, brown sugar, powdered sugar and vanilla and mix at medium-high speed until creamed, about 2 minutes. Set aside.

Make the cookie dough: In your stand mixer fitted with the paddle attachment, or a large bowl using a handheld mixer, combine the granulated sugar and butter. Mix at high speed until fluffy. Scrape the mixture from the sides and paddle/beaters with a rubber spatula, then mix until fully incorporated. This is complete when your mixture is light, fluffy and off-white. Add the eggs, egg yolks and vanilla paste, then mix until combined.

Into a separate bowl, sift together your flour, cornstarch, salt, baking powder and baking soda, then add the flour mixture to your wet mixture in three parts, making sure to scrape the bowl before each dry addition, to clear the butter from the sides of the bowl. Cover your bowl with plastic wrap and chill in the refrigerator for 30 minutes, or until the dough is cold but still shapeable. While the dough is chilling, preheat the oven to 375°F (190°C). Line two baking sheets with parchment paper.

You can separate the chilled dough into eight equal-sized balls or use a kitchen scale and weigh them all to about 6 ounces (170 g) each. Place 3 inches (8 cm) apart on the prepared pans and bake for 10 to 12 minutes, or until they reach your ideal firmness. Remove from the oven. Let them rest on the pans for 10 to 15 minutes, or until cool.

Spread the crème brûlée topping on each cookie. Sprinkle a generous amount of granulated sugar over the topping. Using a kitchen torch, toast the top of each cookie until it has a nice, crispy brown brûléed top.

WHITE CHOCOLATE-STUFFED MACADAMIA

Yields 7 to 8 giant cookies

The perfect macadamia nut cookie is moist (yeah, I know you hate that word. I don't care), made with two extracts and packed with the perfect balance of nuts to white chocolate. What could make this experience even more mouthwatering? Filling it with even more white chocolate that melts out of the middle when you crack it open. This is a chewy, nutty cookie with almond and vanilla flavors that's stuffed with surprises just waiting to be eaten.

Cookie Dough

¾ cup (150 g) granulated sugar

¾ cup (169 g) light brown sugar

1 cup (2 sticks [227 g]) unsalted butter, at room temperature

2 large eggs

1 large egg yolk

1 tsp vanilla extract

1 tsp almond extract

3½ cups (438 g) all-purpose flour

2 tbsp (16 g) cornstarch

1 tsp iodized salt

1 tbsp (14 g) baking powder

1 tsp baking soda

1 cup (135 g) chopped macadamia nuts

½ cup (88 g) white chocolate chips

Center

2 (4-oz [115 g]) bars white chocolate (I use Ghirardelli®)

Make the cookie dough: In a stand mixer fitted with the paddle attachment, or a large bowl using a handheld mixer, combine the granulated sugar, brown sugar and butter. Mix at medium-high speed until creamed, about 2 minutes. Scrape the mixture from the sides and paddle/beaters with a rubber spatula, then mix until fully incorporated. Add the eggs and egg yolk, vanilla and almond extracts, then mix until just combined.

Into a separate bowl, sift together your flour, cornstarch, salt, baking powder and baking soda and add the flour mixture to your wet mixture in three parts. Make sure to scrape the bowl before each dry addition to clear the butter from the sides of the bowl. Turn off your mixer and, using a rubber spatula, fold in your macadamia nuts and white chocolate chips.

Cover your bowl with plastic wrap and chill in the refrigerator for 30 minutes, or until the dough is cold but still shapeable. While the dough is chilling, preheat the oven to 375°F (190°C). Line two baking sheets with parchment paper.

Add the center: You can separate the chilled dough into eight equal-sized balls or use a kitchen scale and weigh them all to about 6 ounces (170 g) each. Using a large spoon or your fingers, press into the middle of your cookie dough ball to create a small space into which to place the white chocolate. Place two squares of white chocolate in the depression you made in the dough. Pinch the cookie dough closed around the center, rolling it into a smooth ball between your palms. Repeat to fill all the dough balls.

Place four or five filled dough balls 3 inches (8 cm) apart on the prepared pans and lightly press on the tops of each dough ball. Bake your cookies for 12 to 14 minutes, or until they have beautiful, golden-brown edges. Remove from the oven. Let them rest on the pans for 10 to 15 minutes before serving.

MARSHMALLOW-STUFFED FRUITY FUNFETTI

Yields 7 to 8 giant cookies

If the months of testing cookies for this book taught me anything, it's that nothing excites two eight-year-olds like a bright blue, birthday cake–flavored, marshmallow-stuffed, fruity cereal–coated cookie. Too much for your refined palate? Maybe. But to my kids, it's my life's greatest accomplishment.

Cookie Dough

1½ cups (300 g) granulated sugar

¾ cup (1½ sticks [170 g]) unsalted butter, at room temperature

2 large eggs

2 large egg yolks

2 tsp (10 ml) cake batter extract (available from bakery supply shops or online)

3 to 4 drops blue gel food coloring

4 cups (500 g) all-purpose flour

¼ cup (32 g) cornstarch

1 tsp iodized salt

1 tbsp (14 g) baking powder

1 tsp baking soda

½ cup (18 g) Fruity Pebbles or similar cereal

Center

8 Jet-Puffed Marshmallow Bites Birthday Cake Flavored Coated Marshmallows™

For Rolling

2 cups (72 g) Fruity Pebbles or similar cereal

Make the cookie dough: In a stand mixer fitted with the paddle attachment, or a large bowl using a handheld mixer, combine the sugar and butter. Mix at medium-high speed until creamed, about 2 minutes. Scrape the mixture from the sides and paddle/beaters with a rubber spatula, then mix until fully incorporated. Add the eggs, egg yolks and cake batter extract, then mix until just combined. Add the blue food coloring and mix until incorporated.

Into a separate bowl, sift together your flour, cornstarch, salt, baking powder and baking soda, then add the flour mixture to your wet mixture in three parts, making sure to scrape the bowl before each dry addition, to clear the butter from the sides of the bowl. When your dough is mixed, fold in the fruity cereal. Cover your bowl with plastic wrap and chill in the refrigerator for 30 minutes, or until the dough is cold but still shapeable. While the dough is chilling, preheat the oven to 375°F (190°C). Line two baking sheets with parchment paper.

Add the center: You can separate the chilled dough into eight equal-sized balls or use a kitchen scale and weigh them all to about 6 ounces (170 g) each. Using a large spoon or your fingers, press into the middle of each cookie dough ball to create a small space into which to place one marshmallow. Then, fold the surrounding cookie dough around the marshmallow and roll back into a ball. Repeat to fill the other dough balls. Roll each ball in the Fruity Pebbles.

Place four or five filled dough balls 3 inches (8 cm) apart on the prepared pans and lightly press on the tops of each one. Bake your cookies for 12 to 14 minutes, or until they reach your ideal firmness. Remove from the oven. Let rest on the pans for 10 to 15 minutes, then serve.

CHAPTER 5:
ALL AB●UT BUTTER

Salted butter. Butterscotch. Browned butter. Peanut butter. Cookie butter. Stuffed, creamed or browned—whatever your preference, they're all right here. If you didn't know already, butter is the heart of baking and essential to bringing the world's favorite flavors to life. Without butter, there is no caramel, cake or (most important) *cookies*. In this chapter, you'll experience butter in all its best forms.

BROWNED BUTTER CRINKLE

Yields
8 giant
cookies

Browning butter takes it a step beyond melting and adds a toasted, slightly caramelized and nutty flavor. A browned butter cookie may not sound like an exotic combination, but this simple blend of flavors feels like a hug in the mouth.

Cookie Dough
¾ cup (1½ sticks [170 g]) unsalted butter, at room temperature, cut into slices

½ cup (100 g) granulated sugar

1 cup (225 g) light brown sugar

2 large eggs

2 large egg yolks

2 tsp (10 ml) vanilla extract

4 cups (500 g) all-purpose flour

3 tbsp (24 g) cornstarch

1 tbsp (7 g) ground cinnamon

1 tsp iodized salt

1 tsp baking powder

1 tsp baking soda

For Rolling
1 cup (220 g) brown sugar

In a small saucepan, melt the butter over medium heat while stirring constantly. The butter will bubble and eventually turn foamy. Continue to cook, stirring, until it turns a golden amber color, 5 to 7 minutes. Remove the pan from the heat and allow it to cool.

In a stand mixer fitted with the paddle attachment, or a large bowl using a handheld mixer, combine the granulated sugar, brown sugar and the browned butter. Mix at medium-high speed until creamed, about 2 minutes. Scrape the mixture from the sides and paddle/beaters with a rubber spatula, then mix until fully incorporated.

Add the eggs, egg yolks and vanilla, then mix until combined.

Into a separate bowl, sift together your flour, cornstarch, cinnamon, salt, baking powder and baking soda, then add the flour mixture to your wet mixture in three parts, making sure to scrape the bowl before each dry addition, to clear the butter from the sides of the bowl.

Cover your bowl with plastic wrap and chill in the refrigerator for 30 minutes, or until the dough is cold but still shapeable. While the dough is chilling, preheat the oven to 375°F (190°C). Line two baking sheets with parchment paper. Place the brown sugar in a shallow bowl.

You can separate the chilled dough into eight equal-sized balls or use a kitchen scale and weigh them all to about 6 ounces (170 g) each. Roll each cookie in the brown sugar and place 3 inches (8 cm) apart on the prepared pans, giving each a gentle push on top to secure them to the parchment. Bake for 12 to 14 minutes, or until they reach your ideal firmness. Remove from the oven. Let cool on the pans for 10 to 15 minutes before serving.

ALMOND BUTTER BUDDY

This cookie is made with a hint of delicious almond paste and stuffed with almond butter that melts out of the center when you crack it open.

Center
1 cup (256 g) almond butter

Cookie Dough
½ cup (100 g) granulated sugar

¾ cup (169 g) light brown sugar

1 cup (2 sticks [227 g]) unsalted butter, at room temperature

2 large eggs

1 large egg yolk

½ cup (128 g) almond butter

1 tsp almond paste

3½ cups (438 g) all-purpose flour

2 tbsp (16 g) cornstarch

1 tsp iodized salt

1 tsp baking powder

1 tsp baking soda

Make the center: Fill eight 1-ounce (29-ml) wells of a silicone mold with almond butter and freeze until solid. Keep frozen until you are ready to fill your cookies.

Make the cookie dough: In a stand mixer fitted with the paddle attachment, or a large bowl using a handheld mixer, combine the granulated sugar, brown sugar and butter. Mix at medium-high speed for 2 minutes, or until light and fluffy.

Add the eggs, egg yolk, almond butter and almond paste, then mix until combined.

Into a separate bowl, sift together your flour, cornstarch, salt, baking powder and baking soda, then add the flour mixture to your wet mixture in three parts, making sure to scrape the bowl before each dry addition, to clear the butter from the sides of the bowl.

Cover your bowl with plastic wrap and chill in the refrigerator for 30 minutes, or until the dough is cold but still shapeable. While the dough is chilling, preheat the oven to 375°F (190°C). Line two baking sheets with parchment paper.

Add the center: Separate the chilled dough into eight to ten equal-sized balls of dough. Flatten each dough ball in your palm and place your frozen almond butter in the center. Cover the frozen puck of almond butter completely until you have sealed it entirely in cookie dough. You don't want to leave any cracks that the almond butter can seep out of!

Place them 3 inches (8 cm) apart on the prepared pans and bake for 10 to 12 minutes, or until they reach your ideal firmness. Remove from the oven. Let them rest on the pans for about 10 minutes, then serve.

COOKIE BUTTER–FILLED COOKIES

Yields 8 giant cookies

Cookies, coffee plus cookie butter = one of the most delicious combinations I've ever produced. If I was forced to pick a favorite child, this would be a contender.

Center
8 tbsp (120 g) cookie butter, preferably Biscoff® brand

Cookie Dough
1 tbsp (15 ml) vanilla extract

1 tbsp (15 g) granulated instant coffee

1½ cups (300 g) granulated sugar

¾ cup (1½ sticks [170 g]) unsalted butter, at room temperature

2 large eggs

1 large egg yolk

4 cups (500 g) all-purpose flour

¼ cup (32 g) cornstarch

1 tsp iodized salt

2 tsp (9 g) baking powder

2 tsp (9 g) baking soda

2 tsp (5 g) ground cinnamon

1 cup (120 g) crushed Biscoff or similar cookies

Make the center: For any stuffed cookie recipe, it's essential that your center doesn't leak out of the sides! Start by spooning about 1 tablespoon (15 g) of the cookie butter into a ball (I like to use a small, clamping cookie scooper) and place on a plate. This can be easier if you freeze your cookie butter for a few hours before scooping. Once you have a plate of your cookie butter center spheres, place the plate in the freezer until your dough is prepared.

Make the cookie dough: In a small bowl, mix together your vanilla and instant coffee and set aside to let the coffee dissolve.

In a stand mixer fitted with the paddle attachment, or a large bowl using a handheld mixer, combine the sugar and butter. Mix at medium-high speed until creamed, about 2 minutes. Scrape the mixture from the sides and paddle/beaters with a rubber spatula and mix until fully incorporated. This is complete when your mixture is light, fluffy and off-white.

Add the eggs, egg yolk and coffee mixture, then mix until just combined.

Into a separate bowl, sift together your flour, cornstarch, salt, baking powder, baking soda and cinnamon, then add the flour mixture to your wet mixture in three parts, making sure to scrape the bowl before each dry addition, to clear the butter from the sides of the bowl.

Once your dough is totally combined, toss in your crushed cookies, and mix for just a few seconds to incorporate them.

(continued)

COOKIE BUTTER–FILLED COOKIES (CONTINUED)

Preheat the oven to 375°F (190°C). Line two baking sheets with parchment paper.

Add the center: You can separate the chilled dough into eight equal-sized balls or use a kitchen scale and weigh them all to about 6 ounces (170 g) each. Place a dough ball in your palm and push it into a bowl shape with your fingers. Place a frozen cookie butter ball in the center of your dough and then firmly close the dough, totally covering your cookie butter. I like to give my cookies a firm rolling between my palms so I'm sure they're totally sealed.

Place 3 inches (8 cm) apart on the prepared pans, then bake for 12 to 14 minutes, or until they reach your ideal firmness. Remove from the oven. Let your cookies rest on the pans for 5 to 10 minutes before serving.

STUFFED PB & J

Yields 8 giant cookies

When I was a kid, my mother used to make me peanut butter and jelly sandwiches with a twist—she grilled them. She did the same for my little sister 20 years later. It taught me that you can get creative with your favorite foods and that taking it a step further can be a whole new experience. This is a giant cookie twist on a childhood favorite—a cakey, peanut butter–packed cookie dough with a classic grape jelly center.

Cookie Dough

1½ cups (300 g) granulated sugar

¾ cup (169 g) light brown sugar

¼ cup (½ stick [57 g]) unsalted butter, at room temperature

2 large eggs

1 large egg yolk

¾ cup (192 g) creamy peanut butter

3½ cups (438 g) all-purpose flour

¼ cup (32 g) cornstarch

1 tsp iodized salt

1 tsp baking powder

1 tsp baking soda

Make the cookie dough: In a stand mixer fitted with the paddle attachment, or a large bowl using a handheld mixer, combine the granulated sugar, brown sugar and butter. Mix at medium-high speed until creamed, about 2 minutes. Scrape the mixture from the sides and paddle/beaters with a rubber spatula and mix until fully incorporated and fluffy.

Add the eggs, egg yolk and peanut butter, then mix until just combined.

Into a separate bowl, sift together your flour, cornstarch, salt, baking powder and baking soda, then add the flour mixture to your wet mixture in three parts, making sure to scrape the bowl before each dry addition, to clear the butter from the sides of the bowl.

Cover your bowl with plastic wrap and chill in the refrigerator for 30 minutes, or until the dough is cold but still shapeable. While the dough is chilling, preheat the oven to 375°F (190°C). Line two baking sheets with parchment paper. Place the granulated sugar for rolling in a shallow bowl.

(continued)

Center

10.5 oz (300 g) Concord grape jelly

For Rolling

1 cup (200 g) granulated sugar

Add the center: You can separate the chilled dough into eight equal-sized balls or use a kitchen scale and weigh them all to about 6 ounces (170 g) each. Place a dough ball in your palm and push it into a bowl shape with your fingers. Using a spoon or a #100 cookie scoop, place a scoop of jelly in the depression you made in the dough. Tightly pinch the cookie dough closed around the center (don't let the jelly escape during baking!), rolling it into a smooth ball between your palms. Repeat to fill all the dough balls.

Roll the cookies in the granulated sugar and place them 3 inches (8 cm) apart on the prepared pans, giving them each a light push to secure them to the parchment. Bake for 12 to 15 minutes, or until they reach your ideal firmness. Remove from the oven. Let them rest on the pans for about 10 minutes before digging in.

DEATH BY BUTTERSCOTCH

Yields 8 giant cookies

If you ask me, butterscotch is a wildly underrated flavor. It always brings up memories of the smooth taste of Butterbeer from Universal Studios and crunchy no-bake cookies made from melted butterscotch chips and peanut butter at Christmas time. This cookie has a signature, creamy flavor you'll find bursting out of the dough and from the butterscotch ganache center.

Center

1 (11-oz [310-g]) bag butterscotch morsels (I use Nestlé® brand)

2 tbsp (32 g) creamy peanut butter

Cookie Dough

½ cup (100 g) granulated sugar

1 cup (225 g) light brown sugar

¾ cup (1½ sticks [170 g]) unsalted butter, at room temperature

2 large eggs

2 large egg yolks

2 tsp (10 ml) vanilla extract

4 cups (500 g) all-purpose flour

3 tbsp (24 g) cornstarch

1 tsp ground cinnamon

1 tsp iodized salt

1 tsp baking powder

1 tsp baking soda

1 cup (175 g) butterscotch chips

Make the center: In a microwave-safe bowl, melt together the butterscotch morsels and peanut butter in increments of 15 to 30 seconds, stirring between each heating. Once smooth, pour the mixture into eight 1-ounce (29-ml) wells of a silicone mold and freeze until solid.

Make the cookie dough: In a stand mixer fitted with the paddle attachment, or a large bowl using a handheld mixer, combine the granulated sugar, brown sugar and butter. Mix at medium-high speed until creamed, about 2 minutes. Scrape the mixture from the sides and paddle/beaters with a rubber spatula and mix until fully incorporated. This is complete when your mixture is light, fluffy and off-white. Add the eggs, egg yolks and vanilla, then mix until just combined.

Into a separate bowl, sift together your flour, cornstarch, cinnamon, salt, baking powder and baking soda, then add the flour mixture to your wet mixture in three parts, making sure to scrape the bowl before each dry addition, to clear the butter from the sides of the bowl. Turn off the mixer and, using a rubber spatula, fold the butterscotch chips into the dough. Cover your bowl with plastic wrap and chill in the refrigerator for 30 minutes, or until the dough is cold but still shapeable. Preheat the oven to 375°F (190°C). Line two baking sheets with parchment paper.

Add the center: You can separate the chilled dough into eight equal-sized balls or use a kitchen scale and weigh them all to about 6 ounces (170 g) each. Place a dough ball in your palm and push it into a bowl shape with your fingers. Place a frozen butterscotch puck in the center of your dough and then firmly close the dough, totally covering your butterscotch. I like to give my cookies a firm rolling between my palms so I'm sure they're totally sealed. Place 3 inches (8 cm) apart on the prepared pans.

Bake for 12 to 14 minutes, or until they reach your ideal firmness. Remove from the oven. Let your cookies rest on the pans for 10 to 15 minutes before serving.

CHAPTER 6: PACKED WITH PIE

Pies always make me think of celebrations: the first fruit pies of spring, an apple pie at a summer backyard party, gathering with family and friends over the pumpkin pie at Thanksgiving and eating leftover pecan pie in the kitchen with my husband after the Christmas mayhem has passed.

To me, pie is love. It's quite literally a labor of love that requires the perfect crust, filling and baking, but when made into cookie form, it's *so* much simpler for all the same wonderful flavor. I put that same love into each of these giant cookie recipes, a little window into what I love most about cookies, flavor and family.

CARAMEL APPLE PIE COOKIES

Yields 8 giant cookies

When I debuted this cookie to my foolproof taste testers, my BluffCakes team, it became a weekly conversation. "Are we adding the apple pie cookie to the menu? Are you going to make more to test? Can you give me the recipe?" Nothing makes me prouder than knowing this gooey, cinnamon, caramel apple–packed cookie took a chokehold of my team, especially my leader, Jose.

Center

1 (20-oz [567-g]) can apple pie filling

Cookie Dough

1½ cups (300 g) granulated sugar

¾ cup (1½ sticks [170 g]) unsalted butter, at room temperature

2 large eggs

1 large egg yolk

1 tsp caramel emulsion (available from bakery supply shops or online)

4 cups (500 g) all-purpose flour

¼ cup (32 g) cornstarch

1 tsp iodized salt

2 tsp (9 g) baking powder

2 tsp (9 g) baking soda

2 tsp (5 g) ground cinnamon

½ cup (96 g) caramel chips

Make the center: Into each of eight 1-ounce (29-ml) wells of a silicone mini cupcake pan, spoon about 2 tablespoons (30 ml) of apple pie filling. Sometimes cutting the apple slices down a bit can help them fit. Place in the freezer for 2 to 3 hours. You'll want to make sure your apple pie filling pucks are nice and frozen before putting them in your finished cookie dough.

Make the cookie dough: In a stand mixer fitted with the paddle attachment, or a large bowl using a handheld mixer, combine the sugar and butter. Mix at medium-high speed until creamed, about 2 minutes. Scrape the mixture from the sides and paddle/beaters with a rubber spatula and mix until fully incorporated. This is complete when your mixture is light, fluffy and off-white.

Add the eggs, egg yolk and caramel emulsion, then mix until just combined.

Into a separate bowl, sift together your flour, cornstarch, salt, baking powder, baking soda and cinnamon, then add the flour mixture to your wet mixture in three parts, making sure to scrape the bowl before each dry addition, to clear the butter from the sides of the bowl.

Turn off the mixer, toss in your caramel chips and, using a rubber spatula, mix for just a few seconds to incorporate them.

(continued)

CARAMEL APPLE PIE COOKIES (CONTINUED)

For Rolling

1 cup (200 g) granulated sugar

1 tbsp (7 g) ground cinnamon

Preheat the oven to 375°F (190°C). Line two baking sheets with parchment paper. To make your cinnamon sugar, stir together the sugar and cinnamon in a shallow bowl.

Add the center: You can separate the chilled dough into eight equal-sized balls or use a kitchen scale and weigh them all to about 6 ounces (170 g) each. Place a dough ball in your palm and push it into a bowl shape with your fingers. Place a frozen apple pie filling puck in the center of your dough and then firmly close the dough, totally covering your apple pie filling. I like to give my cookies a firm rolling between my palms so I'm sure they're totally sealed.

Roll each filled dough ball in cinnamon sugar and place 3 inches (8 cm) apart on the prepared pans. Place in the fridge for 15 to 20 minutes, then bake for 12 to 14 minutes, or until they are nice and golden on all sides. Remove from the oven. Let your cookies rest on the pans for 5 to 10 minutes, then serve.

PEACH COBBLER COOKIES

Yields 6 to 8 giant cookies

Moving to the Deep South as a teen introduced me to a world of new foods, especially when it comes to baking. Peach cobbler is one of the best things to happen to me, and I was thrilled to put my cookie twist on it.

Filling

1 (15-oz [425-g]) can peaches

1 tbsp (14 g) noniodized salted butter, at room temperature

½ cup (100 g) granulated sugar

Pinch of ground cinnamon

¼ cup (32 g) cornstarch

1 tsp vanilla extract

Cookie Dough

1½ cups (300 g) granulated sugar

¾ cup (1½ sticks [170 g]) unsalted butter, at room temperature

2 large eggs

2 large egg yolks

2 tsp (10 ml) vanilla extract

Make the filling: Drain your canned peaches into a bowl, separating the peaches from their juice. In a saucepan, combine your drained peach juice, butter, sugar, cinnamon and cornstarch, and whisk over medium-high heat until the mixture thickens. Meanwhile, chop the peaches. Once the juice mixture reaches a good, thick consistency, add your chopped peaches and the vanilla, and stir over the heat for a few more minutes. Remove from the heat and let cool.

Into each of eight 1-ounce (29-ml) wells of a silicone cupcake pan, spoon the peach filling until each well is about half-full. Sometimes cutting the peach slices down a bit can help them fit. Place in the freezer for 2 to 3 hours. You'll want to make sure your peach cobbler filling pucks are nice and frozen before putting them in your finished cookie dough.

Make the cookie dough: In a stand mixer fitted with the paddle attachment, or a large bowl using a handheld mixer, combine the sugar and butter. Mix at medium-high speed until creamed, about 2 minutes. Scrape the mixture from the sides and paddle/ beaters with a rubber spatula and mix until fully incorporated. This is complete when your mixture is light, fluffy and off-white.

Add the eggs, egg yolks and vanilla, then mix until just combined.

(continued)

PEACH COBBLER COOKIES (CONTINUED)

4 cups (500 g) all-purpose flour

¼ cup (32 g) cornstarch

1 tsp iodized salt

1 tsp baking powder

1 tsp baking soda

1 tsp ground cinnamon

½ cup (8 g) freeze-dried peaches, crushed

For Rolling

1 cup (200 g) granulated sugar

1 tbsp (7 g) ground cinnamon

Into a separate bowl, sift together your flour, cornstarch, salt, baking powder, baking soda, cinnamon and freeze-dried peaches, then add the flour mixture to your wet mixture in three parts, making sure to scrape the bowl before each dry addition, to clear the butter from the sides of the bowl.

Preheat the oven to 375°F (190°C). Line two baking sheets with parchment paper. To make your cinnamon sugar, stir together the sugar and cinnamon in a shallow bowl.

Add the filling: You can separate the chilled dough into eight equal-sized balls or use a kitchen scale and weigh them all to about 6 ounces (170 g) each. Place a dough ball in your palm and push it into a bowl shape with your fingers. Place a frozen peach pie filling puck in the center of your dough and then firmly close the dough, totally covering your peach pie filling. I like to give my cookies a firm rolling between my palms so I'm sure they're totally sealed.

Roll each filled dough ball in cinnamon sugar and place 3 inches (8 cm) apart on the prepared pans. Place in the fridge for 15 to 20 minutes, then bake for 12 to 14 minutes, or until they are nice and golden on all sides. Remove from the oven. Let your cookies rest for 5 to 10 minutes before lifting from the pans.

PUMPKIN PIE COOKIES

Yields 8 giant cookies

Every year, I take pride in gloating that when we met, my husband insisted he hated pumpkin pie—that was until he ate mine. He complained it was always too sweet, too pumpkin-y, too mushy, yada yada yada. The perfect pumpkin pie requires the right balance of spices to pumpkin and a great crust. With this recipe, you skip the hassle of making and rolling pie crust and swap it for a buttery sugar cookie. Enjoy a taste of the day I made my husband eat his words.

Filling

1 (30-oz [850-g]) can pumpkin pie filling

2 large eggs

⅔ cup (160 ml) evaporated milk

Cookie Dough

1½ cups (300 g) granulated sugar

¾ cup (1½ sticks [170 g]) unsalted butter, at room temperature

2 large eggs

2 large egg yolks

2 tsp (10 ml) vanilla extract

4 cups (500 g) all-purpose flour

2 tsp (12 g) iodized salt

2 tsp (9 g) baking powder

2 tsp (9 g) baking soda

¼ cup (32 g) cornstarch

Make the filling: In a medium-sized bowl, mix the pumpkin pie filling, eggs and evaporated milk, then set aside.

Make the cookie dough: In a stand mixer fitted with the paddle attachment, or a large bowl using a handheld mixer, combine the sugar and butter. Mix at medium-high speed until creamed, about 2 minutes. Scrape the mixture from the sides and paddle/beaters with a rubber spatula and mix until fully incorporated. This is complete when your mixture is light, fluffy and off-white. Add the eggs, egg yolks and vanilla, then mix until combined.

Into a separate bowl, sift together your flour, salt, baking powder, baking soda and cornstarch, then add the flour mixture to your wet mixture in three parts, making sure to scrape the bowl before each dry addition, to clear the butter from the sides of the bowl.

Cover your bowl with plastic wrap and chill in the refrigerator for 30 minutes, or until the dough is cold but still shapeable. While the dough is chilling, preheat the oven to 375°F (190°C). Line two baking sheets with parchment paper.

(continued)

PUMPKIN PIE COOKIES (CONTINUED)

Optional Toppings

1 large egg

2 tbsp (30 ml) water

Granulated sugar, for sprinkling

You can separate the chilled dough into 16 equal-sized balls (to create eight giant sandwich cookies) or use a kitchen scale and weigh them all to about 3 ounces (85 g) each. Take your cookie dough balls and flatten each into a disk about ½ inch (1.3 cm) thick and 3 to 4 inches (8 to 10 cm) in diameter, placing half of the disks 3 inches (8 cm) apart on the prepared pans. These will be the base of your "cookie pie." Once all eight bases are laid flat on the pans, use a #100 cookie scoop or a spoon to place a dollop of pumpkin pie mixture in the center of each.

Take the remainder of your flattened cookie dough disks and gently lay one on top of each pumpkin-topped disk. Next, using your fingers or the tip of a fork, crimp the edges of your cookies to give them that pretty "pie" finished look. Finally, I like to cut an X into the center of each top disk.

If you wish, mix 1 egg with 2 tablespoons (30 ml) of water to create an egg wash, and rub across the top of each cookie with either your fingers or a pastry brush. This will give your cookie a buttery and shiny finish just like the top of a classic double-crust pie. Sprinkle each with sugar.

Bake for 10 to 12 minutes, or until they reach your ideal golden pie-like color. Remove from the oven. Let them rest for about 10 minutes before lifting from the pans.

SWEET POTATO PIE COOKIES

Yields 8 giant cookies

This recipe is a cross between a classic southern sweet potato pie and a stuffed cookie. It wasn't until I moved to the South as a teenager that I was even introduced to the age-old southern family tradition that is sweet potato pie. Here in our hometown of Memphis, it's a staple of every holiday season that you can find at every bakery, grocery store and good southern mother's dinner table. Sweet potato pie is all about the best southern home cooking with sugar, spices and sweet potatoes, only this version is wrapped in a cozy sugar cookie.

Filling

15 oz (425 g) canned or cooked sweet potatoes or yams

¼ cup (60 ml) sweetened condensed milk

1 tsp ground cinnamon

½ tsp freshly grated nutmeg

¼ cup (60 g) light brown sugar

Cookie Dough

1½ cups (300 g) granulated sugar

¾ cup (1½ sticks [170 g]) unsalted butter, at room temperature

2 large eggs

2 large egg yolks

2 tsp (10 ml) vanilla extract

4 cups (500 g) all-purpose flour

2 tsp (12 g) iodized salt

2 tsp (9 g) baking powder

2 tsp (9 g) baking soda

¼ cup (32 g) cornstarch

1 tsp ground cinnamon

1 tsp freshly grated nutmeg

Make the filling: In a food processor, pulse the sweet potatoes, sweetened condensed milk, cinnamon, nutmeg and brown sugar until smooth. Set aside.

Make the cookie dough: In a stand mixer fitted with the paddle attachment, or a large bowl using a handheld mixer, combine the granulated sugar and butter. Mix at medium-high speed until creamed, about 2 minutes. Scrape the mixture from the sides and paddle/beaters with a rubber spatula and mix until fully incorporated and fluffy.

Add the eggs, egg yolks and vanilla, then mix until combined.

Into a separate bowl, sift together your flour, salt, baking powder, baking soda, cornstarch, cinnamon and nutmeg, then add the flour mixture to your wet mixture in three parts, making sure to scrape the bowl before each dry addition, to clear the butter from the sides of the bowl.

Cover your bowl with plastic wrap and chill in the refrigerator for 30 minutes, or until the dough is cold but still shapeable. While the dough is chilling, preheat the oven to 375°F (190°C). Line two baking sheets with parchment paper.

(continued)

Optional Toppings

1 large egg

2 tbsp (30 ml) water

Granulated sugar, for sprinkling

Cinnamon, for sprinkling

You can separate the chilled dough into 16 equal-sized balls (to create eight giant sandwich cookies) or use a kitchen scale and weigh them all to about 3 ounces (85 g) each. Take your cookie dough balls and flatten each into a disk ½ inch (1.3 cm) thick and 3 to 4 inches (8 to 10 cm) in diameter, placing half of the disks 3 inches (8 cm) apart on the prepared pans. This will be the base of your "cookie pie." Once all eight bases are laid flat on the pans, use a #100 cookie scoop or a spoon to place a dollop of the sweet potato mixture in the center of each.

Take the remainder of your flattened cookie dough disks and gently lay one on top of each sweet potato–topped cookie. Next, using your fingers or the tip of a fork, crimp the edges of your cookies to give them that pretty "pie" finished look. Finally, I like to cut an X into the center.

If you wish, mix 1 egg with 2 tablespoons (30 ml) of water to create an egg wash, and rub across the top of each cookie with either your fingers or a pastry brush. Sprinkle each with granulated sugar and cinnamon.

Bake for 10 to 12 minutes, or until they reach your ideal golden pie-like color. Remove from the oven. Let them rest on the pans for about 10 minutes, then serve.

BLUEBERRY COBBLER COOKIES

Yields 6 to 8 giant cookies

Blueberry cobbler is one of my favorite childhood comfort treats. My mother was never an avid baker, but with some fruit, sugar and biscuit mix, she could make cobbler magic. This fruity, stuffed cobbler cookie gives me a taste of that memory. It can be topped with ice cream, even more blueberries, or you can swap out the blueberries for your choice of delicious assorted berries. The opportunities are endless.

Filling
1 (21-oz [595-g]) can blueberry pie filling

Cookie Dough
1½ cups (300 g) granulated sugar

¾ cup (1½ sticks [170 g]) unsalted butter, at room temperature

Zest of 1 lemon

2 large eggs

2 large egg yolks

2 tsp (10 ml) vanilla extract

3½ cups (438 g) all-purpose flour

¼ cup (32 g) cornstarch

1 tsp iodized salt

1 tsp baking powder

1 tsp baking soda

¾ cup (105 g) dried blueberries

Crumble
¼ cup (55 ml) melted unsalted butter

½ cup (115 g) light brown sugar

Zest of two lemons

½ cup (60 g) all-purpose flour

Make the filling: Fill eight 1-ounce (29-ml) wells of a silicone mold with the blueberry pie filling. Place in the freezer until they're fully frozen. Reserve the rest of the filling for garnish.

Make the cookie dough: In a stand mixer fitted with the paddle attachment, or a large bowl using a handheld mixer, combine the granulated sugar and butter. Mix at medium-high speed until creamed, about 2 minutes. Scrape the mixture from the sides and paddle/beaters with a rubber spatula, then mix until fully incorporated.

Add the lemon zest, eggs, egg yolks and vanilla, then mix until just combined.

Into a separate bowl, whisk together your flour, cornstarch, salt, baking powder, baking soda and dried blueberries, then add the flour mixture to your wet mixture in three parts, making sure to scrape the bowl before each dry addition to clear the butter from the sides of the bowl.

Cover your bowl with plastic wrap and chill in the refrigerator for 30 minutes, or until the dough is cold but still shapeable. While the dough is chilling, preheat the oven to 375°F (190°C). Line two baking sheets with parchment paper.

Make the crumble: In a medium-sized bowl, combine the melted butter, brown sugar, lemon zest and flour and mix well with a spoon. Set aside.

You can separate the chilled dough into eight equal-sized balls or use a kitchen scale and weigh them all to about 6 ounces (170 g) each. Place a dough ball in your palm and push it into a bowl shape with your fingers. Place one portion of the frozen blueberry pie filling in the depression you made in the dough. Pinch the cookie dough closed around the center, rolling it into a smooth ball between your palms. Repeat to fill all the dough balls.

Place the filled dough balls 3 inches (8 cm) apart on the prepared pans and press a generous amount of crumble onto the top of each cookie. Bake for 12 to 15 minutes, or until they reach your ideal golden color. After pulling them from the oven, spoon some of the remaining blueberry pie filling and drizzle onto the top. Let cool on the pans for 10 to 15 minutes, then enjoy!

CHAPTER 7: COFFEE, SPICE & EVERYTHING NICE

Some people wake up first thing in the morning, well rested with no need to reach for a cup of coffee. I, on the other hand, have a countertop sprawling with sugars, spices and a stainless-steel espresso machine to keep my addiction on tap.

Coffee isn't just fuel for me. Having the freedom to mix such combinations as brown sugar and cinnamon syrup, almond milk, a dash of heavy cream and two shots of espresso is a ritual, not just a necessity. These flavors and recipes reflect my love for sugar, spice and that stainless-steel espresso machine I will be buried with.

GIANT SNICKERDOODLE

Yields 8 giant cookies

This isn't your grandma's snickerdoodle recipe . . . it's mine. Much love to my great-grandmother Agnes, for unintentionally passing this classic recipe down to me (yes, I took a picture of her recipe card when I was 19 and never lost it—sorry, Agnes). But I make it as big as your hand and full of classic sugar and cinnamon flavor. The Giant Snickerdoodle is everything you love about snickerdoodles but BIGGER.

Cookie Dough

1½ cups (300 g) granulated sugar

¾ cup (1½ sticks [170 g]) unsalted butter, at room temperature

2 large eggs

2 large egg yolks

2 tsp (10 ml) vanilla extract

4 cups (500 g) all-purpose flour

¼ cup (32 g) cornstarch

2 tsp (12 g) iodized salt

2 tsp (9 g) baking powder

2 tsp (9 g) baking soda

2 tsp (5 g) ground cinnamon

For Rolling

1 cup (200 g) granulated sugar

1 tbsp (7 g) ground cinnamon

Make the cookie dough: In a stand mixer fitted with the paddle attachment, or a large bowl using a handheld mixer, combine the sugar and butter. Mix at medium-high speed until creamed, about 2 minutes. Scrape the mixture from the sides and paddle/beaters with a rubber spatula and mix until fully incorporated. This is complete when your mixture is light, fluffy and off-white.

Add the eggs, egg yolks and vanilla, then mix until just combined.

Into a separate bowl, sift together your flour, cornstarch, salt, baking powder, baking soda and cinnamon, then add the flour mixture to your wet mixture in three parts, making sure to scrape the bowl before each dry addition, to clear the butter from the sides of the bowl.

Cover your bowl with plastic wrap and chill in the refrigerator for 30 minutes, or until the dough is cold but still shapeable. While the dough is chilling, preheat the oven to 375°F (190°C). Line two baking sheets with parchment paper. To make your cinnamon sugar, stir together the sugar and cinnamon in a shallow bowl.

You can separate the chilled dough into eight equal-sized balls or use a kitchen scale and weigh them all to about 6 ounces (170 g) each. Roll each cookie in the cinnamon sugar. Place 3 inches (8 cm) apart on the prepared pans and bake for 10 to 12 minutes, or until they reach your ideal firmness. Remove from the oven. Let them rest on the pans for about 10 minutes before digging in.

CHOCOLATE CHURRO COOKIES

Yields 8 giant cookies

This cookie is inspired by the countless Costco trips made just a little bit sweeter by the end-of-shopping treat: the jumbo churro. I'm sure plenty of people would consider the Costco churro a "serves two" treat, but that's just for quitters. This is my giant cookie version of that churro, rolled in cinnamon sugar and bursting with a chocolate center.

Center
1 (13-oz [371-g]) jar chocolate hazelnut spread (I use Nutella)

Cookie Dough
½ cup (100 g) granulated sugar

1 cup (225 g) light brown sugar

¾ cup (1½ sticks [170 g]) unsalted butter, at room temperature

2 large eggs

2 large egg yolks

2 tsp (10 ml) vanilla extract

4 cups (500 g) all-purpose flour

¼ cup (32 g) cornstarch

2 tsp (12 g) iodized salt

2 tsp (9 g) baking powder

2 tsp (9 g) baking soda

1 tbsp (7 g) ground cinnamon

For Rolling
1 cup (200 g) granulated sugar

1 tbsp (7 g) ground cinnamon

Chill the center: Place your chocolate hazelnut spread jar in the freezer. This will stiffen the spread so it's ready to scoop later.

Make the cookie dough: In a stand mixer fitted with the paddle attachment, or a large bowl using a handheld mixer, combine the granulated sugar, brown sugar and butter. Mix at medium-high speed until creamed, about 2 minutes. Scrape the mixture from the sides and paddle/beaters with a rubber spatula and mix until fluffy and creamed.

Add the eggs, egg yolks and vanilla, then mix until combined.

Into a separate bowl, sift together your flour, cornstarch, salt, baking powder, baking soda and cinnamon, then add the flour mixture to your wet mixture in three parts, making sure to scrape the bowl before each dry addition, to clear the butter from the sides of the bowl.

Cover your bowl with plastic wrap and chill in the refrigerator for 30 minutes, or until the dough is cold but still shapeable. While the dough is chilling, preheat the oven to 375°F (190°C). Line two baking sheets with parchment paper. To make the cinnamon sugar, stir together the granulated sugar and cinnamon in a shallow bowl.

Add the center: You can separate the chilled dough into eight equal-sized balls or use a kitchen scale and weigh them all to about 6 ounces (170 g) each. Place a dough ball in your palm and push it into a bowl shape with your fingers. Using a spoon or a #100 cookie scooper, scoop dollops of the chilled chocolate hazelnut spread and drop into the depression you made

in the dough. Pinch the cookie dough closed around the center, rolling it into a smooth ball between your palms. Repeat to fill all the dough balls.

Roll each filled dough ball in the cinnamon sugar and place 3 inches (8 cm) apart on the prepared pans. Bake for 10 to 12 minutes, or until they reach your ideal firmness. Remove from the oven. Let them rest on the pans for about 10 minutes before serving.

GIANT COFFEEDOODLE

Yields 8 giant cookies

My morning ritual, like many people's, begins with coffee. I require a copious amount of coffee as many times a day as I can swing. To me, coffee isn't just an adrenaline boost; it's a flavor, a schedule, a way of starting my day with my best foot forward. This recipe has instant coffee to give the strongest kick of coffee-ness. If you're a real coffee lover, add even more.

Cookie Dough

1 tbsp (15 g) granulated instant coffee

1 tsp vanilla extract

1 tsp coffee emulsion (available from bakery supply shops or online)

1 tbsp (15 ml) water

1½ cups (300 g) granulated sugar

¾ cup (1½ sticks [170 g]) unsalted butter, at room temperature

2 large eggs

2 large egg yolks

4 cups (500 g) all-purpose flour

¼ cup (32 g) cornstarch

2 tsp (12 g) iodized salt

2 tsp (9 g) baking powder

2 tsp (9 g) baking soda

2 tsp (5 g) ground cinnamon

For Rolling

1 cup (200 g) granulated sugar

1 tbsp (7 g) ground cinnamon

In a small bowl, mix together the instant coffee, vanilla, coffee emulsion and water, then set aside.

In a stand mixer fitted with the paddle attachment, or a large bowl using a handheld mixer, combine the sugar and butter. Mix at medium-high speed until creamed, about 2 minutes. Scrape the mixture from the sides and paddle/beaters with a rubber spatula and mix until fully incorporated. This is complete when your mixture is light, fluffy and off-white.

Add the eggs, egg yolks and the coffee mixture, then mix until just combined.

In a separate bowl, sift together your flour, cornstarch, salt, baking powder, baking soda and cinnamon, then add the flour mixture to your wet mixture in three parts, making sure to scrape the bowl before each dry addition to clear the butter from the sides of the bowl.

Cover your bowl with plastic wrap and chill in the refrigerator for 30 minutes, or until the dough is cold but still shapeable. While the dough is chilling, preheat the oven to 375°F (190°C). Line two baking sheets with parchment paper. To make your cinnamon sugar, stir together the sugar and cinnamon in a shallow bowl.

You can separate the chilled dough into eight equal-sized balls or use a kitchen scale and weigh them all to about 6 ounces (170 g) each. Roll each ball in the cinnamon sugar. Place 3 inches (8 cm) apart on the prepared pans and bake for 10 to 12 minutes, or until they reach your ideal firmness. Remove from the oven. Let them rest on the pans for about 10 minutes, then serve.

CARAMEL-STUFFED ESPRESSO CHUNK

Yields 7 to 8 giant cookies

Coffee and chocolate are a match made in heaven. If you love both, this recipe will blow your mind. This is an espresso cookie with chunks of chopped dark chocolate stuffed with chewy salted caramel in the center.

Cookie Dough

¾ cup (1½ sticks [170 g]) unsalted butter, at room temperature

½ cup (100 g) granulated sugar

1 cup (225 g) light brown sugar

2 large eggs

2 large egg yolks

¼ cup (60 g) instant espresso powder

4 cups (500 g) all-purpose flour

3 tbsp (24 g) cornstarch

1 tsp iodized salt

1 tsp baking powder

1 tsp baking soda

1 cup (175 g) chopped dark chocolate

Center

7 oz (198 g) salted caramels (I prefer Shotwell Candy Co.)

For Topping

Flaky salt, for sprinkling

Make the cookie dough: First, brown your butter. In a small saucepan, heat the butter over medium heat. It will begin to bubble and then foam. Be careful to whisk constantly to avoid burning. After a few minutes, your butter will brown and turn a nice amber color. Transfer the butter to a medium-sized bowl and set aside until it is cool enough to touch.

In a stand mixer fitted with the paddle attachment, or a large bowl using a handheld mixer, combine the granulated sugar, brown sugar and browned butter. Mix at medium-high speed until creamed, about 2 minutes. Scrape the mixture from the sides and paddle/beaters with a rubber spatula and mix until fully incorporated. Add the eggs, egg yolks and espresso powder, then mix until just combined.

In a separate bowl, sift together your flour, cornstarch, salt, baking powder and baking soda, then add the flour mixture to your wet mixture in three parts, making sure to scrape the bowl before each dry addition, to clear the butter from the sides of the bowl. Turn off the mixer and, using a rubber spatula, fold in the chopped chocolate.

Cover your bowl with plastic wrap and chill in the refrigerator for 30 minutes, or until the dough is cold but still shapeable. While the dough is chilling, preheat the oven to 375°F (190°C). Line two baking sheets with parchment paper.

Add the center: You can separate the chilled dough into eight equal-sized balls or use a kitchen scale and weigh them all to about 6 ounces (170 g) each. Using a large spoon or your fingers, press into the middle of a cookie dough ball to create a small space into which to place one or two caramels. Then, fold the surrounding cookie dough around the caramel(s) and roll back into a ball. Repeat to fill the remaining dough balls.

Place four or five filled dough balls 3 inches (8 cm) apart on the prepared pans and lightly press on the top of each dough ball. Bake your cookies for 12 to 14 minutes, or until they have beautiful, golden-brown edges. Remove from the oven and lightly sprinkle with the flaky salt. Let them rest for 10 to 15 minutes before lifting from the pans.

CHAPTER 8:
FRUITY
FLAVOR

Fruits always brings me back to my earliest days of baking, farmers' market trips with my mother and letting the fruits that I found in season inspire my baking. In pies, cakes, tarts, muffins, breads and, of course, cookies, fruits of all kinds lend some of the brightest, most powerful flavors to baked dishes.

The recipes in this chapter are inspired by some of my favorite childhood memories: running around in the Florida heat in springtime, chasing down an ice cream truck for a Creamsicle™ or eating my weight in strawberries in the back seat of my mom's car after the Florida Strawberry Festival. In this chapter, you'll find cookie versions of both of those memories as well as a white chocolate–packed Key lime cookie (page 119) and more. Fruit tastes like home.

KEY LIME DREAM COOKIES

Each year, my husband insists on having the perfect Key lime pie in place of a birthday cake. So, what makes the perfect Key lime pie? Zesty lime, a balance of sweet and tart, creamy whipped vanilla and that perfectly baked golden flavor. All of these are balanced in this giant cookie with just the right amount of Key lime flavor, white chocolate and fresh lime zest. It's almost good enough to replace Cookie Daddy's annual treat (his words, not mine).

1½ cups (300 g) granulated sugar

¾ cup (1½ sticks [170 g]) unsalted butter, at room temperature

2 large eggs

2 large egg yolks

Zest of 2 limes

2 tsp (10 ml) Key lime extract

4 to 5 drops neon green gel food coloring

4 cups (500 g) all-purpose flour

1 tsp iodized salt

1 tsp baking powder

1 tsp baking soda

¼ cup (32 g) cornstarch

1 cup (175 g) white chocolate chips

In a stand mixer fitted with the paddle attachment, or a large bowl using a handheld mixer, combine the sugar and butter. Mix at medium-high speed until creamed, about 2 minutes. Scrape the mixture from the sides and paddle/beaters with a rubber spatula and mix until fully incorporated. This is complete when your mixture is light, fluffy and off-white.

Add the eggs, egg yolks, lime zest and Key lime extract, then mix until just combined. Pause your mixer and add four to five drops of green gel food color. Mix until the color is fully incorporated.

Into a separate bowl, sift together your flour, salt, baking powder, baking soda and cornstarch, then add the flour mixture to your wet mixture in three parts. Make sure to scrape the bowl before each dry addition, to clear the butter from the sides of the bowl.

Turn off your mixer and, using a rubber spatula, fold in your white chocolate chips.

Cover your bowl with plastic wrap and chill in the refrigerator for 30 minutes, or until the dough is cold but still shapeable. While the dough is chilling, preheat the oven to 375°F (190°C). Line two baking sheets with parchment paper.

You can separate the chilled dough into eight equal-sized balls or use a kitchen scale and weigh them all to about 6 ounces (170 g) each. Place 3 inches (8 cm) apart on the prepared pans and bake for 10 to 12 minutes, or until they reach your ideal firmness. Remove from the oven. Let them rest on the pans for about 10 minutes before digging in.

GIANT DREAMSICLE COOKIES

A nostalgic beach day frozen treat: The Dreamsicle™! What started as a wacky cookie idea brainstorm ended in one of the best cookie flavor discoveries of BluffCakes' history. I shared a favorite childhood memory with my team, my love for my home state of Florida and the orange-filled treats my family shared in the sweltering heat of the Sunshine State. Any good Florida child knew that if you were lucky enough to catch the ice cream truck, the Creamsicle was the king of summer treats. We casually spoke about how so many childhood memories could be translated to cookies, and there the Giant Dreamsicle Cookie was born: bright, zesty orange and creamy white chocolate flavor with a pop of color.

1½ cups (300 g) granulated sugar

¾ cup (1½ sticks [170 g]) unsalted butter, at room temperature

2 large eggs

2 large egg yolks

2 tsp (10 ml) orange emulsion (available from bakery supply shops or online)

2 to 3 drops Chefmaster® insta-gel® orange food coloring

4 cups (500 g) all-purpose flour

¼ cup (32 g) cornstarch

2 tsp (12 g) iodized salt

2 tsp (9 g) baking powder

2 tsp (9 g) baking soda

1 cup (175 g) white chocolate chips

Zest of 1 orange

In a stand mixer fitted with the paddle attachment, or a large bowl using a handheld mixer, combine the sugar and butter. Mix at medium-high speed until creamed, about 2 minutes. Scrape the mixture from the sides and paddle/beaters with a rubber spatula and mix until fully incorporated. This is complete when your mixture is light, fluffy and off-white.

Add the eggs, egg yolks and orange emulsion, then mix until just combined. Add 2 to 3 drops of your gel food coloring and mix into your wet ingredients on low speed until the mixture reaches your desired shade of bright orange—the color brings all the fun to this cookie!

Into a separate bowl, sift together your flour, cornstarch, salt, baking powder and baking soda, then add the flour mixture to your wet mixture in three parts, making sure to scrape the bowl before each dry addition to clear the butter from the sides of the bowl.

Turn off your mixer and, using a rubber spatula, fold in your white chocolate chips and orange zest.

Cover your bowl with plastic wrap and chill in the refrigerator for 30 minutes, or until the dough is cold but still shapeable. While the dough is chilling, preheat the oven to 375°F (190°C). Line two baking sheets with parchment paper.

You can separate the chilled dough into eight equal-sized balls or use a kitchen scale and weigh them all to about 6 ounces (170 g) each. Place 3 inches (8 cm) apart on the prepared pans. Bake for 12 to 14 minutes, or until they reach your ideal firmness. Remove from the oven. Let your cookies rest on the pans for 5 to 10 minutes, then serve.

LEMON BLUEBERRY COOKIES

Yields 8 giant cookies

Who turned a zesty blueberry muffin into a cookie? Me. If ever there were a cookie to eat for breakfast, this is the one. But life is short so, honestly, that should be any cookie. If you really want this cookie to be a showstopper, one thing is not optional: the sugary topping.

Cookie Dough

1½ cups (300 g) granulated sugar

¾ cup (1½ sticks [170 g]) unsalted butter, at room temperature

2 large eggs

1 large egg yolk

2 tsp (10 ml) lemon emulsion (available from bakery supply shops or online)

Zest of 2 lemons

½ cup (78 g) frozen blueberries

4 cups (500 g) all-purpose flour

¼ cup (32 g) cornstarch

1 tsp iodized salt

1 tsp baking powder

1 tsp baking soda

For Rolling

½ cup (100 g) granulated sugar

½ cup (60 g) powdered sugar

In a stand mixer fitted with the paddle attachment, or a large bowl using a handheld mixer, combine the granulated sugar and butter. Mix at medium-high speed until creamed, about 2 minutes. Scrape the mixture from the sides and paddle/beaters with a rubber spatula and mix until fully incorporated. This is complete when your mixture is light, fluffy and off-white.

Add the eggs, egg yolk, lemon emulsion, lemon zest and frozen blueberries, then mix until just combined.

Into a separate bowl, sift together your flour, cornstarch, salt, baking powder and baking soda, then add the flour mixture to your wet mixture in three parts, making sure to scrape the bowl before each dry addition, to clear your wet ingredients from the sides of the bowl.

Cover your bowl with plastic wrap and chill in the refrigerator for 20 minutes, or until the dough is cold but still shapeable. While the dough is chilling, preheat the oven to 375°F (190°C) and line two baking sheets with parchment paper. Combine your granulated and powdered sugar in a shallow bowl.

You can separate the chilled dough into eight equal-sized balls or use a kitchen scale and weigh them all to about 6 ounces (170 g) each. Roll each ball in the sugar mixture before placing them about 3 inches (8 cm) apart on the prepared pans. Bake for 12 to 14 minutes, or until they reach your ideal firmness. Remove from the oven. Let your cookies rest for about 10 minutes before lifting from the pans.

STRAWBERRY DREAMS

Strawberries always bring me back to childhood memories of eating my weight in the world's freshest strawberries at the Florida Strawberry Festival. The stomachache was worth it every time. These cakey cookies are packed with that strawberry flavor that made fighting the sweltering Florida heat survivable year after year.

Cookie Dough

1½ cups (300 g) granulated sugar

¾ cup (1½ sticks [170 g]) unsalted butter, at room temperature

½ cup (8 g) freeze-dried strawberries

1 large egg

1 large egg yolk

2 tbsp (14 g) dry strawberry-flavor gelatin mix (I use Jell-O® brand)

¼ cup (60 ml) pureed strawberries

2 to 3 drops Chefmaster insta-gel pink coloring

4 cups (500 g) all-purpose flour

¼ cup (32 g) cornstarch

1½ tsp (9 g) iodized salt

1½ tsp (7 g) baking powder

1½ tsp (7 g) baking soda

For Rolling

½ cup (60 g) sifted powdered sugar

In a stand mixer fitted with the paddle attachment, or a large bowl using a handheld mixer, combine the granulated sugar and butter. Mix at medium-high speed until creamed, about 2 minutes. Scrape the mixture from the sides and paddle/beaters with a rubber spatula and mix until fully incorporated. This is complete when your mixture is light, fluffy and off-white.

While your butter and sugar are mixing, take your freeze-dried strawberries and, using a blender or food processor, process them until you have a fine powder. Set aside.

Add the egg, egg yolk, strawberry gelatin mix and pureed strawberries to the butter mixture, then mix until just combined. Add 2 to 3 drops of your gel food coloring and mix into the wet mixture on low speed until it reaches your desired shade of bright pink—the color will settle into a more subtle pink later due to the real pureed strawberry.

Into a separate bowl, sift together your flour, cornstarch, reserved freeze-dried strawberry powder, salt, baking powder and baking soda, then add the flour mixture to your wet mixture in three parts, making sure to scrape the bowl before each dry addition, to clear the butter from the sides of the bowl.

Cover your bowl with plastic wrap and chill in the refrigerator for 30 minutes, or until the dough is cold but still shapeable. While the dough is chilling, preheat the oven to 375°F (190°C). Line two baking sheets with parchment paper. Place the powdered sugar in a shallow bowl.

You can separate the chilled dough into eight equal-sized balls or use a kitchen scale and weigh them all to about 6 ounces (170 g) each. Roll each cookie in the powdered sugar and place 3 inches (8 cm) apart on the prepared pans, giving each one a gentle push with your palm to secure it to the parchment. Bake for 12 to 14 minutes, or until they reach your ideal firmness. Remove from the oven. Let your cookies rest on the pans for 5 to 10 minutes, then serve.

RASPBERRY DELIGHT

Yields 8 to 9 giant cookies

It was my husband who first introduced me to the infamous Subway raspberry white chocolate cookies. I'm supposed to believe a sandwich franchise makes the best raspberry cookie you can find? I was doubtful until I literally ate my own words. I put my own spin on my husband's childhood favorite cookie (because I can't have him thinking anyone can do it better than me) and made it giant: raspberries, white chocolate, and bright pink color packed into a chewy cookie.

1½ cups (300 g) granulated sugar

¾ cup (1½ sticks [170 g]) unsalted butter, at room temperature

2 large eggs

2 large egg yolks

2 tsp (10 ml) raspberry emulsion (available from bakery supply shops or online)

2 to 3 drops Chefmaster insta-gel pink gel food coloring

4 cups (500 g) all-purpose flour

¼ cup (32 g) cornstarch

2 tsp (12 g) iodized salt

2 tsp (9 g) baking powder

2 tsp (9 g) baking soda

1 cup (175 g) white chocolate chips

¼ cup (60 ml) muddled raspberries

In a stand mixer fitted with the paddle attachment, or a large bowl using a handheld mixer, combine the sugar and butter. Mix at medium-high speed until creamed, about 2 minutes. Scrape the mixture from the sides and paddle/beaters with a rubber spatula and mix until fully incorporated. This is complete when your mixture is light, fluffy and off-white.

Add the eggs, egg yolks and raspberry emulsion, then mix until just combined. Add 2 to 3 drops of your gel food coloring and mix into the wet mixture on low speed until it reaches your desired shade of bright pink—the color brings all the fun to this cookie!

Sift together your flour, cornstarch, salt, baking powder and baking soda and add the flour mixture to your wet mixture in three parts, making sure to scrape the bowl before each dry addition, to clear the butter from the sides of the bowl.

Turn off your mixer and, using a rubber spatula, fold in your white chocolate chips and muddled raspberries.

Cover your bowl with plastic wrap and chill in the refrigerator for 30 minutes, or until the dough is cold but still shapeable. While the dough is chilling, preheat the oven to 375°F (190°C). Line two baking sheets with parchment paper.

Using your kitchen scale, form the chilled dough into balls anywhere from 6.5 to 6.8 ounces (184 to 193 g), or divide it into eight equal-sized balls. Place at least 3 inches (8 cm) apart on the prepared pans. Bake for 12 to 14 minutes, or until they reach your ideal firmness. Remove from the oven. Let your cookies rest on the pans for 5 to 10 minutes and serve.

PIÑA COLADA COOKIES

Yields 8 giant cookies

Just as the drink does, this cookie brings me back to sunny days, basking in Jamaica with my husband the day after we were married at Sandals South Coast. Pineapple, coconut and a sweet rum glaze top it off.

Rum Pineapple Glaze

⅓ cup (76 g) soft unsalted butter

1 tbsp (15 ml) pineapple juice

2 cups (240 g) powdered sugar

3 tbsp (45 ml) dark rum

Cookie Dough

1½ cups (300 g) granulated sugar

¾ cup (1½ sticks [170 g]) unsalted butter, at room temperature

2 large eggs

2 large egg yolks

1 tsp vanilla extract

¼ cup (60 ml) coconut milk

½ cup (80 g) canned, drained pineapple tidbits (reserve at least 1 tbsp [15 ml] of juice for the glaze)

4 cups (500 g) all-purpose flour

¼ cup (32 g) cornstarch

¼ cup (30 g) sweetened coconut flakes

2 tsp (12 g) iodized salt

2 tsp (9 g) baking powder

2 tsp (9 g) baking soda

1 cup (175 g) white chocolate chips

For Rolling

2 cups (240 g) sweetened coconut flakes

Make the glaze: In a medium-sized bowl, whisk together the butter, pineapple juice, powdered sugar and rum. Set aside.

Make the cookie dough: In a stand mixer fitted with the paddle attachment, or a large bowl using a handheld mixer, combine the granulated sugar and butter. Mix at medium-high speed until creamed, about 2 minutes. Scrape the mixture from the sides and paddle/beaters with a rubber spatula and mix until fluffy.

Add the eggs, egg yolks, vanilla, coconut milk and pineapple tidbits, then mix to combine.

Into a separate bowl, whisk together your flour, cornstarch, sweetened coconut flakes, salt, baking powder and baking soda, then add the flour mixture to your wet mixture in three parts. Make sure to scrape the bowl before each dry addition to clear the butter from the sides of the bowl.

Turn off your mixer and, using a rubber spatula, fold in the white chocolate chips.

Cover your bowl with plastic wrap and chill in the refrigerator for 30 minutes, or until the dough is cold but still shapeable. While the dough is chilling, preheat the oven to 375°F (190°C). Line two baking sheets with parchment paper. Place the coconut flakes for rolling in a shallow bowl.

You can separate the chilled dough into eight equal-sized balls or use a kitchen scale and weigh them all to about 6 ounces (170 g) each. Roll each cookie in the sweetened coconut flakes. Place at least 3 inches (8 cm) apart on the prepared pans and bake for 10 to 12 minutes, or until they reach your ideal firmness. Remove from the oven. Let them rest on the pans for about 10 minutes before drizzling with the glaze.

CRAN ROSEMARY CRINKLE

Yields 8 giant cookies

When it comes to Thanksgiving, cranberry sauce is one of my favorite sides. It's super tart on its own, but sweeten and blend it with the right amount of orange zest and you've got a winning combination.

Cookie Dough

1½ cups (300 g) granulated sugar

Zest of 1 orange

¼ cup (7 g) fresh rosemary leaves

¾ cup (1½ sticks [170 g]) unsalted butter, at room temperature

2 large eggs

2 large egg yolks

2 tsp (10 ml) vanilla extract

4 cups (500 g) all-purpose flour

¼ cup (32 g) cornstarch

2 tsp (12 g) iodized salt

2 tsp (9 g) baking powder

2 tsp (9 g) baking soda

1 cup (120 g) dried cranberries

For Rolling

1 cup (200 g) granulated sugar

½ cup (60 g) sifted powdered sugar

In a food processor, blend your granulated sugar, orange zest and rosemary leaves until the mixture is fragrant and the rosemary has broken up a bit.

In a stand mixer fitted with the paddle attachment, or a large bowl using a handheld mixer, combine the rosemary mixture and the butter. Mix at medium-high speed until creamed, about 2 minutes. Scrape the mixture from the sides and paddle/beaters with a rubber spatula and mix until fully incorporated.

Add the eggs, egg yolks and vanilla, then mix until just combined.

Into a separate bowl, sift together your flour, corn-starch, salt, baking powder and baking soda and add the flour mixture to your wet mixture in three parts, making sure to scrape the bowl before each dry addition, to clear the butter from the sides of the bowl.

Turn off your mixer and, using a rubber spatula, fold in the dried cranberries.

Cover your bowl with plastic wrap and chill in the refrigerator for 30 minutes, or until the dough is cold but still shapeable. While the dough is chilling, preheat the oven to 375°F (190°C). Line two baking sheets with parchment paper.

Stir together the granulated sugar and powdered sugar in a shallow bowl.

You can separate the chilled dough into eight equal-sized balls or use a kitchen scale and weigh them all to about 6 ounces (170 g) each. Roll each cookie in your sugar mixture. Place at least 3 inches (8 cm) apart on the prepared pans and bake for 10 to 12 minutes, or until they reach your ideal firmness. Remove from the oven. Let them rest on the pans for about 10 minutes, then serve.

CHAPTER 8:
WHAT'S
THE TEA?

The truth is, I didn't always love tea. More accurately, I didn't always know how to appreciate it. Marrying a man who doesn't drink caffeine and receiving strict advice from your doctor not to overcaffeinate while pregnant will definitely change that.

I found a love for my morning blueberry matcha latte and my evening raspberry leaf tea. I learned how subtle, sweet and refreshing flavors, such as green tea with a hint of lemon, can be. All the while, my Teddy Bear, Theodore, was growing. I was beginning my giant cookie journey and working my love for teas into the flavors you'll find in these recipes.

THE BIG CHAI

This is a deliciously cozy cookie packed with chai spices. I can never eat one of these without thinking of the Taylor Swift chai cookie craze. Who doesn't want to taste a cookie made by the brilliant mind behind "You Belong with Me"? That craze (and my long-standing love for T-Swizzle) is what inspired this cookie. To trap the chai spice flavors in this recipe, you'll use reduced chai latte concentrate, which can be found in most coffee and tea aisles at your local grocery. I highly recommend borrowing the bourbon glaze from the Maple Bacon Pecan Giant Cookies (page 66) to top it off.

Chai Reduction

1 cup (240 ml) chai latte concentrate

1 tsp ground cinnamon

1½ tsp (3 g) ground cardamom

½ tsp ground cloves

Cookie Dough

½ cup (100 g) granulated sugar

1 cup (225 g) light brown sugar

¾ cup (1½ sticks [170 g]) iodized salted butter, at room temperature

2 large eggs

2 large egg yolks

4 cups (500 g) all-purpose flour

3 tbsp (24 g) cornstarch

1 tsp iodized salt

1 tsp baking powder

1 tsp baking soda

1 tsp ground cinnamon

½ tsp ground cardamom

½ tsp ground cloves

Make your chai reduction: In a small saucepan, bring the chai concentrate, cinnamon, cardamom and cloves to a boil. Once your mixture is boiling, lower the heat to medium-low and let simmer, making sure to stir frequently, for 7 to 10 minutes, or until it has reduced to ¼ cup (60 ml). Set aside to cool.

Make the cookie dough: In a stand mixer fitted with the paddle attachment, or a large bowl using a handheld mixer, combine the granulated sugar, brown sugar and butter. Mix at medium-high speed until creamed, about 2 minutes. Scrape the mixture from the sides and paddle/beaters with a rubber spatula and mix until fully incorporated. This is complete when your mixture is light, fluffy and off-white.

Add the eggs, egg yolks and chai reduction, then mix until just combined.

Into a separate bowl, sift together your flour, cornstarch, salt, baking powder, baking soda, cinnamon, cardamom and cloves, then add the flour mixture to your wet mixture in three parts, making sure to scrape the bowl before each dry addition, to clear the butter from the sides of the bowl.

Cover your bowl with plastic wrap and chill in the refrigerator for 30 minutes, or until the dough is cold but still shapeable. While the dough is chilling, preheat the oven to 375°F (190°C). Line two baking sheets with parchment paper.

You can separate the chilled dough into eight equal-sized balls or use a kitchen scale and weigh them all to about 6 ounces (170 g) each. Place four or five balls 3 inches (8 cm) apart on the prepared pans and lightly press on the top of each dough ball. Bake your cookies for 12 to 14 minutes, or until they have beautiful, golden-brown edges. Remove from the oven. Let them rest on the pans for 10 to 15 minutes before serving.

GREEN TEA WITH LEMON CURD

Yields
8 giant
cookies

Made with real green tea leaves and lemon and stuffed with your choice of homemade lemon curd (my personal favorite is Bonne Maman®): all the comfort of a cup of green tea in a chewy cookie.

Cookie Dough

1½ cups (300 g) granulated sugar

Zest of 2 lemons

6 green tea bags

¾ cup (1½ sticks [170 g]) unsalted butter, at room temperature

2 large eggs

1 large egg yolk

Green gel food coloring (optional)

1 tsp lemon emulsion (available from bakery supply shops or online)

4 cups (500 g) all-purpose flour

¼ cup (32 g) cornstarch

1 tsp iodized salt

1 tsp baking powder

1 tsp baking soda

Center

12.7 oz (360 g) lemon curd

Make the cookie dough: In a food processor, blend your sugar, lemon zest and the contents of the green tea bags until fragrant.

In a stand mixer fitted with the paddle attachment, or a large bowl using a handheld mixer, combine the tea mixture with the butter. Mix at medium-high speed until light and fluffy. Scrape the mixture from the sides and paddle/beaters with a rubber spatula and mix until fully incorporated.

Add the eggs, egg yolk, food coloring (if using) and lemon emulsion, then mix until just combined.

Into a separate bowl, sift together your flour, cornstarch, salt, baking powder and baking soda and add the flour mixture to your wet mixture in three parts, making sure to scrape the bowl before each dry addition, to clear your wet ingredients from the sides of the bowl.

Cover your bowl with plastic wrap and chill in the refrigerator for 20 minutes, or until the dough is cold but still shapeable. While the dough is chilling, preheat the oven to 375°F (190°C). Line two baking sheets with parchment paper.

Add the center: You can separate the chilled dough into eight equal-sized balls or use a kitchen scale and weigh them all to about 6 ounces (170 g) each. Place a dough ball in your palm and push it into a bowl shape with your fingers. Using a spoon or a #100 cookie scoop, place a scoop of lemon curd in the depression you made in the dough. Tightly pinch the cookie dough closed around the center (you don't want the lemon curd to escape during baking), rolling it into a smooth ball between your palms. Repeat to fill all the dough balls.

Place the filled dough balls 3 inches (8 cm) apart on the prepared pans, giving them each a light push to secure them to the parchment. Bake for 12 to 15 minutes, or until they reach your ideal firmness. Remove from the oven. Let them rest for about 10 minutes before lifting from the pans.

MATCHA PASSION FRUIT

Yields
8 giant
cookies

This cookie is a chewy, sweet vessel of one of my favorite iced drinks: a matcha latte. It is a light, matcha-flavored cookie with a natural green color that's stuffed with pineapple–passion fruit preserves.

Cookie Dough

1½ cups (300 g) granulated sugar

Zest of 2 lemons

¾ cup (1½ sticks [170 g]) unsalted butter, at room temperature

2 large eggs

1 large egg yolk

1 tsp lemon emulsion (available from bakery supply shops or online)

4 cups (500 g) all-purpose flour

¼ cup (32 g) cornstarch

¼ cup (24 g) matcha green tea powder

1 tsp iodized salt

1 tsp baking powder

1 tsp baking soda

Center

13 oz (370 g) pineapple–passion fruit preserves (I prefer Bonne Maman brand), chilled

Make the cookie dough: In a stand mixer fitted with the paddle attachment, or a large bowl using a handheld mixer, combine the granulated sugar, lemon zest and butter. Mix at medium-high speed for 2 to 3 minutes, until light and fluffy. Scrape the mixture from the sides and paddle/beaters with a rubber spatula and mix until fully incorporated. Add the eggs, egg yolk and lemon emulsion, then mix until just combined.

Into a separate bowl, sift together your flour, cornstarch, matcha powder, salt, baking powder and baking soda, then add the flour mixture to your wet mixture in three parts, making sure to scrape the bowl before each dry addition, to clear your wet ingredients from the sides of the bowl.

Cover your bowl with plastic wrap and chill in the refrigerator for 20 minutes, or until the dough is cold but still shapeable. While the dough is chilling, preheat the oven to 375°F (190°C). Line two baking sheets with parchment paper.

Add the center: You can separate the chilled dough into eight equal-sized balls or use a kitchen scale and weigh them all to about 6 ounces (170 g) each. Place a dough ball in your palm and push it into a bowl shape with your fingers. Using a spoon or a #100 cookie scoop, place a scoop of the chilled preserves in the depression you made in the dough. Tightly pinch the cookie dough closed around the center, rolling it into a smooth ball between your palms. Repeat to fill all the dough balls.

Place the filled dough balls 3 inches (8 cm) apart on the prepared pans, giving them each a light push to secure them to the parchment. Bake for 12 to 15 minutes or until they reach your ideal firmness. Remove from the oven. Let them rest on the pans for about 10 to 15 minutes to prevent them from falling apart.

ACKNOWLEDGMENTS

This book would not have been possible without the support and encouragement of my husband, Tyler, the love of my life. Thank you for standing with me, making my life's dream yours, raising our beautiful children and always believing I can do anything.

Thank you to my BluffCakes Bakery family: Jasmine, Demi, Tasha, Jose, Robin and our quickly growing team. No matter where life takes you, you will all always hold a special place in my heart for the role you played in our story.

Thank you to Mason, my biggest boy, for filling my days with dozens of "I love yous" that I needed more than you know.

Thank you to Charlotte, for being a beautiful, brilliant piece of Jenny Wren I get to hold on to forever.

To Theodore, thank you for being the best thing that ever happened to me. Being your mother is the greatest accomplishment of my life.

Thank you to Marissa, Iris and the incredible team at Page Street Publishing for giving me this life-changing opportunity and working with me to create something I am so deeply proud of.

Finally, thank you to my Cookie Monsters. I never imagined to find myself with an audience of millions cheering me on through this endeavor. You have pushed me through peaks and valleys, and I will always be grateful to you.

ABOUT THE AUTHOR

Chloe Joy Sexton is the owner of BluffCakes Confections, a giant cookie bakery in Memphis, Tennessee, that ships giant flavors all over the world. She began baking at 14 years old and rose to TikTok fame sharing her baking, lifestyle content and humor. *Big Yum* is her first published cookbook. Chloe has been featured in various national talk shows, online publications and celebrity events for custom giant cookies.

She resides in Memphis with her husband and business partner, Tyler, their children Mason and Theodore, and her little sister, Charlotte.

INDEX